11/03

24.⁰⁰

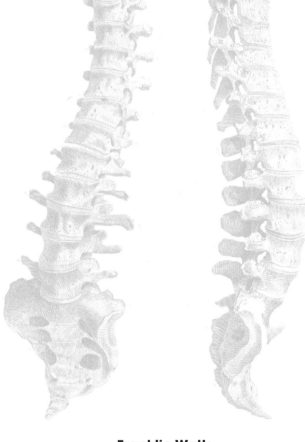

# Vertebrates

Christine Petersen

**Franklin Watts**
A Division of Scholastic Inc.
New York Toronto London Auckland Sydney
Mexico City New Delhi Hong Kong
Danbury, Connecticut

*For Sam and Michael*

Photographs © 2002: Aaron Norman: 30, 38; Animals Animals: 96 (Erwin & Peggy Bauer), 81 right (Joe McDonald), 90 (Charles Palek), 107 (Rich Reid); Earth Scenes/David Dennis: 75; Peter Arnold Inc./Secret Sea Visions/Jones/Shimlock: cover; Photo Researchers, NY: 12 left, 81 left (Tim Davis), 61 (Jeff Greenberg), 12 right (Frans Lanting), 15 top (Pat Lynch), 43, 49, 63 (Tom McHugh), 18 (Hans Reinhard/Okapia), 86 (David Weintraub), 35 (Dr. Paul A. Zahl); Visuals Unlimited: 58 top right (A.J. Copley), 58 bottom (Kevin Copley), 20 (A. Kerstitch), 23, 29, 58 top left (Ken Lucas), 69 (Joe McDonald), 53 (Jim Merli), 100 (Science), 15 inset (Marty Snyderman), 72 (Jerome Wexler); www.arttoday.com: back cover, 1.

Library of Congress Cataloging-in-Publication Data

Petersen, Christine.
    Vertebrates / by Christine Petersen
        p. cm.
Includes bibliographical references (p. ).
Summary: A close look at past and present vertebrates, including fish, birds, amphibians, reptiles, and mammals.
    ISBN 0-531-12020-1
    1. Vertebrates—Juvenile literature. (1. Vertebrates.) 1. Title.
    QL605.3 .P48 2002
    569—dc21

                                                    2001003032

# Contents

## Chapter One: The Science of Life

## Chapter Two: Fishes

## Chapter Three: Amphibians

## Chapter Four: Reptiles

## Chapter Five: Birds

## Chapter Six: Mammals

# THE SCIENCE OF LIFE

Have you ever looked at the world around you and wondered how it all came to be? It's human nature to question life's beginnings. Ancient people told traditional stories to explain the origin of the world and its creatures. Modern religions also seek to solve the riddle of our existence and to determine our place in the world. Science uses logic, observation, and research to address these same mysteries.

## WHY CLASSIFY?

One of the best ways to approach any question—even one as complex as the story of life on Earth—is to look at it piece by piece. To understand the workings of a car's engine, you first have to identify each of its parts and understand how they all work together. The same is true of nature.

The variety of life on Earth, also called *biodiversity*, is remarkable. Scientists have identified 1.5 million *species*, or unique types of organisms, on our planet so far. Countless more remain to be discovered. In total, Earth's biodiversity may include between 5 million and 100 million species—organisms ranging from bacteria to flowering plants, and from jellyfish to great apes. You may wonder how biologists sort out the relationships between so many species. The process is called classification, or *taxonomy* (Greek for "naming groups"). Taxonomy uses the similarities between living things to group them into categories.

Imagine that you have been assigned to explore a deep cave under a Mexican rain forest, a place never before seen by humans. Other members of your research team will map the cave, collect vegetation, take water samples, and describe the rock formations. Your job is to find any *animals* that live in or use the cave. As you explore, you collect samples of the animals you find. You write descriptions of them in your journal and take photographs. Afterward, you must determine if your cave creatures are related to animals outside the cave or whether any of the animals are entirely unknown to science.

As you begin your journey, you find an animal swimming in a stream that flows out of the cave. You scoop it up in a net and observe that the animal has a bony skeleton, scaly skin, gills, and fins. Biologists have already identified these as characteristics that are shared by fishes, so the first level of classification is easy. This fish also has long, whiskerlike projections coming off its face, and it lives near the bottom of the stream. With this much information, you can identify it as a catfish. Later, you find another fish living in the same stream but deep inside the cave, where it is completely dark. This second fish also has whiskers and lives at the stream's bottom, but there is no color or patterning on its skin, and it has no eyes. These features tell you that it is a blind cave catfish. If you look closer, you may find other characteristics that distinguish it even further from other catfishes.

## CLASSIFICATION SYSTEMS

The idea of classifying living things isn't new. About 2,400 years ago the Greek philosopher Aristotle, a dedicated observer of the natural world, imagined a ladder with a plant or animal on each rung. The simplest sat on the bottom rungs, while the most complex had places toward the top. Living things had always held their exact positions on this *scala naturae* ("scale of nature"), Aristotle said, and they always would. Aristotle also grouped

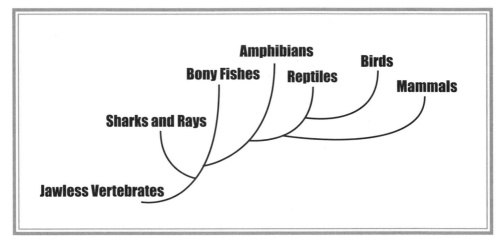

Cladograms are branching diagrams that show evolutionary relationships between living things. This cladogram shows the "family tree" of vertebrate animals.

animals based on their behavior: dolphins and fishes, for example, were classified together because they swim.

In the mid-eighteenth century, a Swedish scientist named Carolus Linnaeus began collecting descriptions and samples of plants and animals from around the world. Basing his system on Aristotle's time-honored one, Linnaeus identified and grouped organisms based on their external features, like leaf shape, scales, fur, and feathers. Each organism was given two names, a *genus* (general name) and a *species name* (a specific name not shared by any other member of the genus). Together, these two words define a species.

Here's how Linnaeus's classification system works. You probably share a last name with your brothers, sisters, and parents (and perhaps some grandparents and cousins, too) because you're all part of the same family. The genus serves a similar function—it's a name shared by organisms that are closely related. *Pteropus*, for example, is the genus of flying foxes—large, fruit-eating bats, about sixty species of which are found in Africa, Asia, and Australia. No other group of animals has this name—it's used only to describe flying foxes. The species name is much like your first name. It tells the members of a genus apart: *Pteropus samoensis* is found on the islands of Samoa, while *Pteropus conspicillatus* is the spectacled flying fox of New Guinea and Australia. You'll notice that scientific names are always written in italics (to show that the words are in a foreign language), with the genus name capitalized and the species name in lower case.

The other great advantage of Linnaean taxonomy is that it crosses all language boundaries. Consider the common mouse. In Japanese, the word for mouse is *nezumi*. In Cherokee, it's tsi-s-de-tsi. In Swedish, it is *råtta*. Thanks to Linnaeus's system, however, there's just one taxonomic name for the common mouse—*Mus musculus*—and it's understood by biologists all over the world.

## FINDING THE THREADS

In taxonomy, each genus belongs to a family, and families are subsets of orders. Orders fit into classes, and classes fit into phyla (the plural of phylum). The largest group is the kingdom, of which five are currently recognized: monerans (single-celled creatures), protists (multicellular, microscopic creatures), fungi, plants, and animals. The taxonomics of our spectacled flying fox, *Pteropus conspicillatus*, looks like this: Family Pteropodidae (Old World flying foxes), Order Chiroptera (bats), Class Mammalia, Phylum Chordata, Kingdom Animalia.

Linnaeus's naming system is still in use today, although our modern definition of "species" has gone far beyond outward appearances. Unlike Aristotle and Linnaeus, we know that species change over time. We've also learned that appearances can be misleading—two species can look and even behave alike, but still be from separate groups.

By today's standards, two individuals are grouped as the same species only if they are able to reproduce in the wild, without human assistance. In addition, their offspring must survive and produce offspring with other members of the same group. Different species, in turn, are considered relatives if they look or

# The Big Picture

Linnaeus, like Aristotle, pictured the world as an unchanging place. Within a few years of Linnaeus's death, however, the idea that species are "set in stone" was challenged.

In the early 1800s geologists—scientists who study Earth's formation and history—realized that our planet's rocky foundations are laid down in layers, like cards in a deck. While digging, geologists began to find something unexpected: impressions of plants and animals embedded in the rock. We now know that many of these *fossils* form when plants or animals die and are covered over with mud or soil. Bones are slowly replaced by minerals, which harden to become part of the surrounding rock. Other signs of ancient life may fossilize, too, if left undisturbed for a long time: footprints, burrows, shells, and teeth are just a few of the items that reveal the presence of creatures that lived long ago.

Those early geologists noticed that some of the fossils looked different from any organism presently alive on Earth. Stranger yet, fossil species—and sometimes even whole groups of species—changed from one rock layer to the next. Here was some of the first evidence that life on Earth had not always been as it is today. The planet was once home to different species that have since disappeared and been replaced.

Over the past 200 years, science has made great strides in decoding Earth's ancient history by studying and comparing fossils with modern species. Rocks contain evidence of the planet's ancient secrets—climate change, the rise and fall of oceans, the eruption of volcanoes, and the erosion of mountain ranges. They also show us the calendar of life itself: *geologic time*, measured not in minutes, hours, or days, but in millions of years.

behave similarly, if their fertilized eggs go through similar stages of development, or when the genetic (chemical) makeup of their cells is similar. All of these characteristics suggest a shared ancestry.

In addition to naming and classifying organisms, biologists seek to explain the history of life on Earth. There are several systems used for this purpose. For example, relationships between species can be diagrammed in *clades*, or biological family trees. The trunk of a clade represents the oldest ancestor in a particular line. Branching points off this main trunk are marked by the appearance of an unusual characteristic that resulted in a new species (or sometimes a whole new group). All of the species on a single branch must possess that new characteristic. Clades and cladograms ("drawings" of family trees) help us visualize the relationships between organisms and, at the same time, reveal the points at which they diverge.

## VARIATIONS ON A THEME

In 1831, 22-year-old Charles Darwin left England with the crew of the H.M.S. *Beagle*, whose mission was to map and survey the lands south of Earth's equator. During the five-year trip, Darwin took on the unofficial role of ship's biologist, collecting specimens of "new" types of plants and animals and keeping a detailed journal of the wonders he encountered along the way. He also studied the ideas of geologists and biologists. Darwin began to believe that Earth was an extremely ancient place and that life on the planet had changed over time. This idea was supported by the variety of species Darwin observed everywhere the *Beagle* traveled. Darwin returned to England full of revolutionary ideas about the causes of biological diversity.

Of particular interest to Darwin was a group of finches he found on the Galápagos Islands, a chain of thirteen volcanic islands and

The beaks of Darwin's finches, thirteen species of which are found on the Galápagos Islands, have evolved as "tools" appropriate to each species's food sources. Left: medium ground finch (*Geospiza fortis*) Right: cactus finch (*Geospiza scandens*)

more than a hundred rocky islets off the western coast of South America. Because the island finches were so similar in appearance to finches he had encountered on the mainland, Darwin reasoned that the islands must have been "colonized" by birds blown off course by storms long ago. The birds had thrived on these islands, where they encountered no predators and few competitors for resources.

In the years after his return to England, Darwin had time to examine his Galápagos finch collection closely. Although the finches looked similar, he noticed one important difference: their beaks. Some were long and narrow. Others were short and sharp. Still others were thick, as are the beaks of parrots. The variation in beaks appeared to be linked to what the birds ate: thick-billed birds could crack even the largest nuts, long-billed birds probed holes in trees for insects, while birds with small beaks could pick up and eat delicate seeds.

Darwin suspected that, on the Galápagos Islands, the most successful birds would be the ones whose beak shape allowed them to eat whatever food was available: large seeds, small seeds, and so forth. Successful birds could pass along their beak structure to their offspring, until eventually a certain beak type would become common. Darwin was convinced that this *natural selection* process, in which the environment determines the direction of change in a species, accounted for the diversity of species we see on Earth today.

Though Darwin's theory of natural selection explained a great deal, he couldn't say how traits are passed along. Darwin didn't know, as modern biologists do, that individuals inherit one set of *genes*, or cellular materials that determine an organism's characteristics, from each of their parents. The combination of these genes provides a chemical plan for the characteristics their offspring will develop. Natural selection "chooses" the genes that are passed along because individuals are more likely to survive and reproduce if their traits suit the current environmental conditions. When the environment changes, different traits may be selected. If a species fails to *evolve*—to change over time—it may be unable to adapt to sudden shifts in its environment. The result may be *extinction*, the disappearance of an entire species.

## ANIMAL BEGINNINGS

Life started from humble beginnings indeed—single-celled bacterial species first appeared nearly 3.5 billion years ago and still exist today. These microscopic creatures made their living by converting sunlight into energy through a process called *photosynthesis*. They may have been simple, but bacteria already had an exceptional adaptation: the ability to reproduce. Some of those simple cells eventually began to join into colonies, which cooperated as multicellular organisms. Unlike their single-celled ancestors, these organisms could use other organisms as a source of energy by eating them.

The first animals, called *invertebrates* (animals without backbones), have been around for more than 600 million years. Many invertebrates became extinct long ago, but others—including sponges, worms, snails, squid, insects, and sea stars—remain with us today and account for more than 95 percent of the animal species on Earth.

For a long time, all animals were invertebrates. Their bodies were soft and flexible, supported only by the water around them. Such creatures could float from place to place or attach themselves to the ocean bottom. Some, like clams, evolved hard shells as protection and support for their delicate internal organs. Others, like crabs, developed hinged suits of armor and were able to walk around freely on the seafloor—and eventually onto land.

## BUILDING A BACKBONE

The story of *vertebrates* (animals with backbones) began 500 million years ago with a rather homely pair of creatures—the lancelets and tunicates.

Lancelets are tiny and look something like tadpoles without heads. The best way to tell one end of a lancelet from the other is to locate the mouth, which is surrounded by a fringe of armlike tentacles that are used to catch food. The tail is a flattened tip that the animal swings back and forth in order to swim. A flexible rod made of *cartilage*, called a notochord, runs like a thin wire down the lancelet's back and gives it support. Just above it lies a nerve cord, which starts near the mouth and ends at the tail. A group of throat slits cover the *gills*, which are used to eat and breathe.

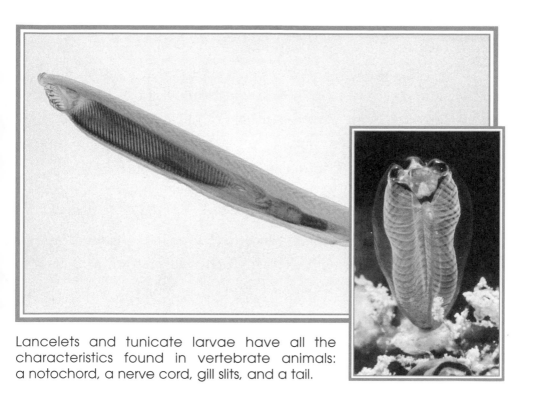

Lancelets and tunicate larvae have all the characteristics found in vertebrate animals: a notochord, a nerve cord, gill slits, and a tail.

The adult tunicate looks like a brightly colored, balloonlike bag with gills. Tunicates attach themselves firmly to rocks, boats, and docks, swaying with the ocean currents and filtering food from the surrounding water. Tunicate *larvae* (the first stage of life out of the egg, which looks different from the adult) are quite different however. They have all the same characteristics as the lancelets: notochord, nerve cord, tail, and gill slits.

It may seem improbable, but those four traits paved the way for a revolution in animal form. They mark the transition between invertebrates and a new lineage of animals advanced enough to occupy every available habitat, whether land, water, or air—the vertebrates.

Vertebrates have highly developed brains that regulate their body functions. The brain also controls sensory organs that give vertebrates exceptional awareness of the world around them through vision, touch, smell, and taste. A line of bony rings, called vertebrae, fit together like pieces of a three-dimensional jigsaw puzzle along the vertebrate's back. These surround and protect the spinal cord and support the animal's body. Spaces between the vertebrae allow smaller nerves to branch off in all directions, increasing sensitivity, reaction time, and motor control.

Vertebrate animals have made good use of their gifts. Today there are more than 50,000 known species of fishes, amphibians, reptiles, birds, and mammals—and they come in a greater range of sizes, shapes, and lifestyles than any other animal group that has ever existed.

# CHAPTER TWO

# F I S H E S

When you look at a globe, it's obvious that much of our planet—more than 70 percent, in fact—is covered with water. Although Earth's oceans, rivers, and lakes may seem as inhospitable to us as outer space, these liquid regions are where life first evolved. Among the most interesting and varied animals in the ocean—and freshwater habitats as well—are the fishes. From tugboat-size whale sharks to tiny gobies, and from speedy tuna to poky seahorses, Earth's watery habitats are filled with the original vertebrates.

## ALL FISHES ARE NOT CREATED EQUAL

All fishes are pretty much the same, right? Wrong! Fishes range in length from one-third of an inch (7.5 millimeters) to 50 feet (15 meters) or more. Some are fierce meat-eaters, while others harmlessly nibble algae from rocks. Some fishes glow like neon lights, while others blend into their surroundings so completely as to seem invisible. And yet other fishes—especially the mysterious residents of the ocean's deepest zones—look like fantasy creatures from a horror film or cartoon.

Whatever their individual styles, all fishes share some basic characteristics. Probably the most obvious is living in water (although we'll meet some exceptions). Fishes are equipped with backbones and internal skeletons, tails, gills, and complex nervous systems—traits we've already learned to recognize as unique to vertebrates. Most fishes are smooth-skinned, with a sleek form that helps them move easily through their liquid world.

Fins are another fishy trait. Although not the exact equivalent of legs, fins serve a similar purpose: to help the animal get around. Each fish has fins specific to its way of life, but most possess a pair of pectoral (shoulder) fins, located on each side of the body behind the head. A pair of pelvic (hip) fins lie near the end of the body. Pelvic and pectoral fins are used like rudders to help the fish steer and remain stable in the water, or to act as brakes. A tail fin at the very end of the body points up and down, providing the thrust for swimming. Dorsal (back) and anal (belly) fins keep the fish from rolling sideways in the water.

Scales are the last common characteristic of fishes. Some scales are made of material like the covering on your teeth, while others are thin, transparent sheets of bone and fiber (similar to your fingernails). One end of the scale is rooted in the skin, and the other end points outward. Scales serve a vital role—they prevent the loss of water from the fish's body into the surrounding environment. In some fishes, scales have even been modified into spiny or thorny weapons.

The lamprey is an ancient species of jawless fish that uses its hose-shaped mouth like a vacuum cleaner to suck up the body fluids of other fishes.

## ANCIENT AGNATHANS

The most primitive fishes are the agnathans, odd creatures bearing only some of the characteristics we associate with modern fishes. Agnathans include the extinct armor-plated fishes, along with lampreys and hagfishes that still live in oceans, lakes, and streams today. Some agnathan fossils date back 500 million years.

Lampreys and hagfishes are missing one thing that's found in all other fishes—jaws. Instead, they have circular mouth openings, like the hose of a vacuum. The hagfish is a scavenger, an oceagoing "trash collector" that eats dead fish. Many lampreys, by contrast, are *parasites*, feeding on living animals and often harming them in the process. A lamprey's mouth is lined with sharp teeth and its tongue is like sandpaper. It attaches itself to the body of another fish, drills a hole in the skin, and makes a meal of the blood.

## MAKE NO BONES ABOUT IT

Next on the fish family tree are the sharks, rays and skates, and chimeras. These are called the cartilaginous fishes because their skeletons are made from rubbery connective tissue (cartilage) instead of rigid bone. There are roughly 750 species of cartilaginous fishes living all over the globe—from the shallow waters around coral reefs and mangrove swamps, to the deep ocean, to the frigid polar regions.

Sharks have been around for more than 400 million years and haven't changed much in all that time. Rays and skates (called "batoid" fishes because their flattened bodies and sweeping pectoral fins look like the wings of a bat) appeared about 200 million years after sharks, and the group includes many graceful species. Most batoid fishes are found in salt water, but a few species survive in rivers as well. The little chimeras (also known as

Manta rays swim by "flapping" their large pectoral fins, which may span 30 feet (9 meters) from tip to tip.

ratfishes), denizens of deep-water environs worldwide, are direct descendants of the shark, and are almost as ancient.

## BONY FISHES

For folks who are fond of fishes, here's some good news: there are more species of bony fishes on the planet today than there are of any other kind of vertebrate—more than 20,000 species. Bony fishes evolved shortly after the sharks, about 360 million years ago, and quickly moved into every aquatic habitat on the planet.

Ray-finned fishes are probably the most familiar to you. Good examples are eels, aquarium fishes like goldfishes and gobies, and commercially important fishes, including tuna and salmon. But lobe-finned fishes and lungfishes are the more ancient varieties. Only one species of lobe-finned fish, the coelacanth, exists today, though this group was fairly common in Earth's ancient past. The name "lobe-fin" comes from the plump fins these fishes use to "walk" along the bottoms of rivers, ponds, and seas. Lungfishes live only in freshwater and have made their homes in swamps and shallow, muddy ponds for hundreds of millions of years. Because there's very little oxygen in the water of such habitats, the lungfish has a second mechanism for breathing: it gulps air through its mouth. Air flows into simple, pouchlike lungs attached to the fish's esophagus (a tube that leads from the throat to the stomach).

Ray-finned fishes include more than 80 percent of the bony fish species. Long, thin bones make their fins almost as flexible as the

# Old Fourlegs

The most famous of all lobe-fins is the coelacanth, an ocean-dwelling species that lives in sea caves as much as 2,500 feet (762 meters) below the surface. Until 1938, scientists knew the coelacanth and its kin only from fossils. They recognized that these fossils were from a very ancient variety of fish that evolved alongside the sharks, but believed that the species had gone extinct 70 to 80 million years ago.

Even though it was assumed to be extinct, Old Fourlegs (as its admirers affectionately call the coelacanth) had become a legend among evolutionary biologists. They had long considered the species, with its large, leglike fins, to be an important evolutionary link between fishes and the four-limbed vertebrates that came onto land 360 million years ago.

As it turns out, coelacanths weren't extinct at all—they were just well hidden. Native South African fishermen had been catching them for centuries.

Since the 1950s, several hundred coelacanths have been found around the Comoros Islands in the Indian Ocean (between Madagascar and Mozambique in eastern Africa). Scientists have used underwater vehicles to visit the coelacanths in their deep water haunts and now know a great deal about their biology and behavior. In 1997 a second population of the species was discovered in Indonesia, thousands of miles from the first group. That's exciting news for scientists who want to protect this living fossil from a real extinction.

fingers of your hands. Attached to joints and muscles, the rays can be moved up and down to alter the shape or width of the fin for better control in swimming. Some male fishes also use their fins to get attention. By fanning them out, the male looks larger and more intimidating to other males trying to invade his territory—and he's more impressive to females. Other fishes use fins as weapons.

Fish-watchers can tell a lot about a fish from the shape and size of its fins. Fast swimmers have long, sharp-pointed, or forked fins. Wide, solid fins suggest the slow movers. Tunneling fish and those that live in rock crevices (like the eels) have very small fins to make movement easier in tight spaces, while racers like the sailfishes have huge fins for balance and thrust.

## JAWS—THEN AND NOW

Armor-plated fishes evolved soon after the lampreys and hagfishes and from the same lineage (though they're now extinct). These large animals had much heavier skulls than agnathans, plus two additional bones: an upper and lower jaw. These created a sturdy framework into which large teeth were firmly set. The upper jaw (attached directly to the skull) provided stability. The lower jaw, hinged to the skull in two places, was flexible and allowed for a strong bite.

Once the jaw became "standard equipment," it began to take on distinct shapes in different fishes, depending upon what they ate. For example, the lower jaw of the deep-sea anglerfish sticks out far beyond the rest of its body, and daggerlike fangs project upward from it. A glowing lure on its head draws prey near, and when they arrive—SNAP! At the other extreme, seahorses and pipefishes have no teeth at all on their long jawbones. Instead, the seahorse uses its pipelike mouth as a straw, sucking floating food (such as baby fish and shrimp) right out of the water.

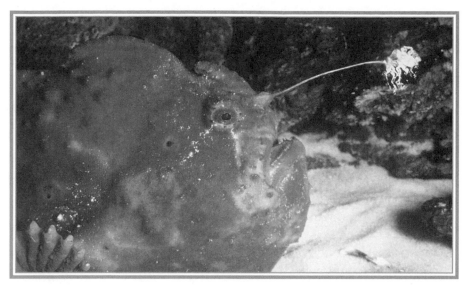

A glow-in-the-dark "fishing lure" extends off the forehead of the deep-sea anglerfish, which lives at depths of 3,000 feet (914 meters) or more.

Elephant-nose fishes have tubular mouths as well, much like the trunks of their namesakes. Their flexible "lips" are used to pluck items out of deep mud in freshwater habitats. The fastest fishes in the world, billfishes (such as marlins and sailfish), have long, swordlike jaws that are probably used in defense and hunting. Wolf fishes have jaws like vices, with gigantic teeth that help them crush the hard shells of mussels and sea urchins. And while giant grouper fishes tend to swallow their prey whole, they, too, have jaws lined with inward-pointing, razorlike teeth.

Sharks take this toothy approach to the limit. Their jaws are lined with rows of saw-edged teeth. As old teeth break or wear down, new ones grow and roll forward to replace them. Yet while most sharks are predatory, whale sharks and basking sharks—the world's largest fishes—are filter-feeders with tiny teeth. They feed by gulping huge mouthfuls of water and using their teeth to strain out tiny floating animals and small fishes.

The mouth of a tropical parrotfish is shaped like a bird's beak, lined with strong teeth that are perfect for nibbling algae off the surface of coral reefs and for biting off hunks of coral skeleton to reach the soft animals within. Hard plates on the roof of the fish's mouth pulverize the rocklike coral into digestible, sand-size pieces that later pass out of the body as waste. The crunching and munching sounds of feeding parrotfishes can be heard for long distances underwater.

## A BREATH OF FRESH-WATER?

Breathing is a vital life process. Oxygen must come into the body, while waste products from hard-working cells (such as the poison gas, carbon dioxide) must be removed. It's easy to understand how this works in air. After all, air is loaded with oxygen and is simple for us to obtain (just take a deep breath!). Breathing in water, on the other hand, is a little different.

You are probably familiar with $H_2O$, better known as the water molecule. What you might not realize is that water molecules don't stay in one piece forever—the bonds that hold the H (hydrogen) and O (oxygen) atoms together are constantly breaking and reforming. As a result, loose hydrogen and oxygen atoms are always present in water along with $H_2O$. They either rebond as water molecules or hook up in pairs as $H_2$ and $O_2$. The $O_2$, called dissolved oxygen, is what fishes "breathe."

Just as you have lungs to pump air through your body, fishes also have a mechanism for gathering $O_2$: gills. Gills are located under flaps of skin on either side of a fish's head. Each set of gills contains four or five clusters of blood red tissue, stacked like the pages of a book and supported by a bony frame. Soft and fleshy like sponges, gills are loaded with microscopic blood vessels called capillaries.

When a fish opens its mouth, water flows through slits in its throat and floods over the gills. The capillaries in the gill tissue absorb dissolved oxygen from the water. Red blood cells transport oxygen inside the capillaries, which flow into larger veins and then to the heart. Fishes have simple hearts with two chambers: one atrium and one ventricle. (By contrast, amphibians and most reptiles have three heart chambers, while mammals and birds have four.) From the atrium of the heart, blood is pumped out to every part of the body.

At the same time the bloodstream is distributing oxygen, it's also collecting carbon dioxide wastes. Once blood reaches the most distant parts of the body, such as the tail, much of its oxygen has been distributed. Deoxygenated blood travels back to the ventricle. From there it's pumped back to the gills. In the gills, carbon dioxide is released into the water, more oxygen is collected, and the cycle begins again.

To make this process work, fishes must always keep water moving across their gills, just as you have to inhale several times a minute. The gill system is incredibly efficient—fishes are able to pull as much as 80 percent of the dissolved oxygen from every mouthful of water.

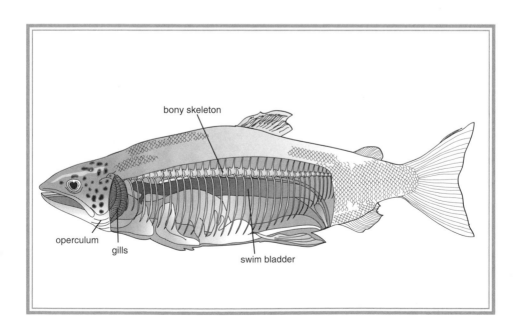

bony skeleton

operculum

gills

swim bladder

## THE HANDY SWIM BLADDER

Do you ever wonder how a fish keeps itself from dropping right to the bottom of the sea? The answer lies in a balloonlike sac called the *swim bladder*, which is attached to the fish's digestive tract. Most bony fishes have them. The swim bladder not only keeps a fish from sinking, it allows the animal to control its depth in the water. By altering the amount of gas in the bladder, a fish can float higher or sink. It can also hover in place effortlessly and conserve energy. To inflate the bladder, a fish may divert oxygen from its bloodstream or take in a mouthful of air from the surface.

Fishes without swim bladders, such as sharks, must move constantly to keep from sinking. Sharks add to their buoyancy by collecting oil in their livers, because oil is lighter than water. Other fishes gulp air and hold it in their stomachs.

## FISH SENSE

Fishes might live in a world radically different from our own, but they are wonderfully equipped to find their way around in it. Like other vertebrates, fishes have a variety of sensory organs that give them information about their world.

Although they don't have external ears like we do, fishes can hear very well. Sounds are sensed as vibrations through their body tissues or swim bladders, traveling along a pathway of bones to the inner ears. Hairs inside the ear chambers are set in swaying motion when sound waves hit them, conveying information to the brain about noises in the water.

Many fishes, particularly the predators, have great senses of smell. When water moves past their nostrils, special scent-detecting cells collect and filter the molecules floating past. Those that suggest food are singled out. By continually sampling the water, a fish can easily follow a scent to its source.

Fishes also use their senses of smell and taste to navigate. Salmon, for example, recognize the "flavor" of the river in which they were born. Each river "tastes" unique, based on the combination of minerals, soil particles, and plants in and around it. Young salmon swim far out to sea and spend years growing and maturing. When they're ready to mate, the adults find their home rivers by tasting the water.

Sharks and some other fishes (including catfishes, rays, electric eels, and elephant-nose fishes) can produce an electrical current from nerve cells in their skin. This current is like a bubble that surrounds the animal. The fish is aware of anything that enters the electric field, allowing the fish to avoid obstacles and locate other animals in the water. Electricity might even be used for communication between the fishes, although scientists are still investigating this. Electricity can also serve as a weapon. Electric eels of the Amazon River in South America produce a charge so strong that it can stun large animals.

Along the sides of some bony fishes, running from head to tail, are two rows of cells. Each cell has a cup-shaped indentation that is lined with sensitive hairs. As the fish moves, water pours over these *lateral lines*. Any disturbance in the water sets the hairs in motion, alerting the fish to activity in its environs—even at a distance and even in total darkness.

## SEEING IS BELIEVING

Eyesight is another important sense for most fishes. Their eyes are much like our own, but they are equipped to deal with the changing patterns of light and dark created when light rays bend through water. Fishes see in color, and it turns out that color plays an important role in their communication.

Colors often serve as identifying marks between members of the same species. The wild color patterns found on many tropical reef fishes may be a way for males and females to locate each other when it comes time to mate. Some fishes use color to warn off competitors. The garibaldi, a small fish of the rocky offshore realms of California, is brilliantly orange. The garibaldi is a fierce defender of its territory and its coloration is a warning to other fishes: stay away!

Colors also serve as an advertisement. Cleaner wrasses are marked with a shimmering blue stripe. Additionally, these aquatic janitors do a dance in the water to tell larger fishes that they are "open for business." This is a wonderful example of a *symbiotic* interaction between species that is beneficial to both. "Clients" approach the wrasse to have parasites, loose skin, and even diseased tissue removed from their bodies. Whatever the wrasse collects, it can eat. Many fishes, like moray eels, will even invite cleaner wrasses to remove parasites from inside their mouths.

## STAYING ALIVE

It may seem a little backward, but many of the riotous colors and patterns worn by fishes are designed to protect them from predators.

You may have noticed that fishes tend to be darker on their backs than on their bellies. This is a color scheme called *countershading*. When seen from below, the pale belly of a fish blends in with the sunlit sky; viewed from above, the fish looks dark and is hard to distinguish from its shadowed surroundings.

Other markings are meant to confuse predators. Some of the colorful butterfly fishes, residents of coral reefs worldwide, bear a large, dark spot near the tail. Looking much like a huge open eye,

Bright orange coloration warns other fishes to stay out of the garibaldi's territory.

the spot is meant to confuse a potential predator into thinking it's facing a much larger opponent than it really is.

The lionfish and scorpion fish bear not only bright stripes that act as *warning coloration*, but also long fins that trail off the body like streamers. If a predator (or careless human) ignores these obvious warning signs, it will meet sharp spines that are loaded with poisons.

Many fishes use *camouflage* as self-protection. They are colored to blend in with their environments. Flatfishes, including flounders and sole, spend most of their lives on or near the ocean floor. Newly hatched flatfishes begin life swimming normally, in an upright position. But as they grow, flatfishes become thinner and thinner. One eye also changes position so that both eyes wind up on the same side of the head. Flatfishes lie sideways under the sand, with only their eyes sticking out to watch the surrounding waters. Special pigment cells under the skin adjust to match the surrounding sand and rocks, making these fishes nearly invisible.

Stonefishes are especially well protected from predators. Their roughened, sand-colored skin camouflages them against the rocky seafloor, and needle-sharp spines contain perhaps the strongest poison found among fishes.

Seahorses are also well camouflaged. The skin color of these tiny creatures closely matches the seaweed or bright corals among which they float. Their relatives, the leafy sea dragons, are named for their leaflike fins that resemble seaweed. Sharks use this strategy, too, producing egg sacs that look deceptively like seaweed.

Stonefishes, perhaps the most deadly poisonous fishes in the world, combine camouflage and poison for an almost perfect defense. By lying in the sand with its rough, sand-colored skin adjusting to match the seafloor, the stonefish is well hidden from predators. And for any unlucky prey passing by, one touch of its needle-sharp spines may mean death. Stingrays, too, are equipped with poison, administered through a wicked 6-inch (15-centimeter) barb at the end of the tail.

All fishes are covered in a layer of mucus, a sticky fluid produced by glands under the skin, which helps them slip though the water more easily. But the mucus on the Moses sole, a flatfish found in the Red Sea, has an extra kick: it contains a shark repellent. Sharks may take a bite, but they'll never repeat the mistake—if they survive.

Hanging out in a crowd is another effective means of avoiding predators, and many fishes take this approach. *Schooling*—coordinated swimming in large groups—is a tactic used by fishes of all sizes, from minnows to tuna. Schooling provides excellent protection because predators find it hard to target individuals among the shimmering, swirling masses.

Of course, many fishes stay alive by using one of the simplest strategies of all time: fleeing and hiding.

## LIVING IN EXTREME ENVIRONMENTS

In the deep sea, where sunlight can never penetrate, fishes are forced to find creative ways to survive. One of the most fascinating approaches is *bioluminescence,* the production of light in living things.

If you could dive down into deep water or swim in the dark of night, you'd be surprised to find that the ocean is not a blanket of darkness. Instead, starry lights seem to break through the water. Animals and microscopic, floating creatures produce these lights by performing chemical reactions. Flashlight fish have large pockets of glowing bacteria below each eye. Green dogfish sharks have tiny organs along the length of their bodies that flash with glowing green chemicals, like landing lights on a runway. This light probably serves two purposes: to startle an unsuspecting predator, and to attract food. Deep-water fishes also tend to have large eyes, helping them spot faint light far in the murky distance.

Underground, the darkness goes unbroken. More than two dozen species of blind cavefishes have been found in the world, living in freshwater rivers and pools that flow through caves and tunnels. These fishes are not only blind, but their eyes are also often completely covered by skin. Instead of eyes, cavefishes have highly sensitive, whiskerlike tentacles on the face, and ridges on the head and back that detect vibrations in the surrounding water. Cavefishes lie still and quiet in the water or move along with slow, silent strokes of their pectoral fins, waiting for signs of other life—and a meal. Because of the fragile nature of their chosen environment, however, many cavefish species are threatened or endangered. They are the victims of water pollution, overfishing, and the careless intrusion of people.

Desert pupfishes are another group of "extreme" fishes. Found in deserts of the American Southwest, pupfishes are challenged by the high temperatures of summer. Short-lived and barely the length of a human finger, pupfishes make their homes in the sandy pools and streams that dot the desert landscape. But as the temperature in summer increases, waterholes begin to dry up. Water temperatures in these little pools can rise as high as 104 degrees Fahrenheit (40 degrees Celsius). Yet some pupfishes always survive to mate, assuring the existence of the next generation. In winter, pupfishes burrow into the loose mud of the pond's bottom to sleep until spring rains fall.

## COLD AS A FISH?

From the iciest polar seas to the warmest tropical reefs, fishes manage to survive. But how do they manage this, with no feathers or fur to insulate them?

Most fishes do not maintain their own body heat, as warm-blooded birds and mammals do. Rather, they (along with amphibians and reptiles) are ectothermic, or cold-blooded. Although this term makes it sound as if a fish's blood runs cold in its veins, it merely means that these fishes don't heat their bodies to a temperature above that of their surroundings.

Ectothermy works because the water around a fish controls its temperature. When water flows across the gills, the blood inside the gills is warmed or cooled to match the temperature of the water. It's something like taking a glass of cold water and one of warm water and mixing them. The result is two cups of water that are the same temperature. As blood makes its way through the body, it warms or cools the muscles along its path. In this way, the fish maintains a temperature that's nearly identical to that of the water surrounding it.

Some of the fastest fishes, like tuna, are not *ectotherms*. Their bodies are warmed by a different kind of heat exchange system. Blood heats up in the hard-working swimming muscles and flows back into the body, side-by-side with arteries containing cool blood from the heart. Along the way, heat is transferred from the veins into the arteries. This strategy keeps the body temperature close to or warmer than the surrounding environment and gives these animals the energy to fuel their active lifestyles.

## HOME AND FAMILY

In fishes, as in all vertebrates, reproduction—mating and the making of a new generation—takes place when a male's sperm cells meet up with the eggs of a female. Fertilization of an egg by a sperm causes a new individual to grow. But as with every other aspect of fish behavior, reproduction takes nearly as many forms as there are species of fishes.

No matter how they go about mating, the eggs of bony fishes are all pretty much alike. The embryo grows inside a soft, balloon-like capsule. The egg also holds a sac of yolk on which the embryo feeds. Hatchling fishes may look like miniature versions of their parents, or may look quite different as larvae before growing into their adult forms.

Most fishes breed only in a particular season, when weather and water temperature are suited to give young fishes a better chance of survival. In tropical waters around the equator, where the conditions are always perfect, fishes may mate at any time of the year. Some fishes always breed in a specific spot and will travel long distances to get there. For instance, salmon and striped bass travel from the sea into rivers and streams. Freshwater eels go just the opposite route, moving from freshwater to the sea to mate.

Among some species, the only act of parenting occurs when the male and female mate. Cod, for example, simply release millions of sperm and eggs into the water to meet randomly. Many of the eggs and larvae don't survive for long but become an important food source for other fishes. The larvae that do survive will never know their parents and must survive on their own.

The male seahorse carries his mate's fertilized eggs inside his belly pouch and gives birth to live young.

# Proud Papas

It all starts with a graceful mating dance. The male and female seahorse swim in slow circles around one another, colors rippling and flashing across their skin. They intertwine their long, coiled tails as if holding hands. This may go on for several days.

Finally, the female swims up face-to-face with the male and releases her eggs into a pouch on his belly, where he fertilizes them. Loaded with several hundred eggs, the full pouch makes the male appear pregnant. All through his "pregnancy," the sea-horse's mate visits him every day.

Once the eggs hatch inside his pouch, the male seahorse goes through something like a birthing labor. His body contracts and he pushes his bulging belly against rocks or coral until the tiny, transparent hatchlings begin to pop out. Within a few days, the hatchlings look like minuscule copies of their parents. The father's responsibility ends there, and the young seahorses must face the watery world on their own.

Some male fishes introduce sperm directly into the female's body, where the eggs develop. Sharks take this route. Female sharks may lay their eggs or keep them inside their bodies and give birth to live young.

A number of species form pair-bonds and raise youngsters together. Some, like the sticklebacks, mudskippers, and jawfishes, carefully prepare nests where the eggs and larvae will be sheltered. Angelfishes situate their eggs on the leaves of water plants. Hatchlings will be watched over by their parents, who protect them as they grow.

The male Siamese fighting fish expends a great deal of energy building his nest. He gulps water bubbles from the surface and deposits them in a foamy clump that is anchored to a plant. Once he attracts a female and her eggs are fertilized, the male fighting fish rudely encourages his mate to "get lost." He then collects "his" eggs inside the bubbly nest and will defend them with his life until the young can swim off on their own.

The male arawana, which lives in the Amazon rain forest, holds his mate's fertilized eggs in his mouth for a month, where the embryos grow, develop, and hatch in safety. The arawana is such an attentive father that he stops eating to make room for his hatchlings. As they grow, the young will leave dad's mouth for a short time each day to feed—but dad will not rest until he's gathered every stray back into his mouth at day's end.

## AND THE STORY CONTINUES

Fish are remarkable survivors. Yet their mark on the world goes beyond their own wonderful diversity. Lob-fins and lungfishes ventured into Earth's shallow waters and swamps 360 million years ago, and something remarkable happened: some learned to live on land. All other vertebrate animals (amphibians, reptiles, birds, and mammals) owe their evolution to these pioneers.

# CHAPTER THREE

# AMPHIBIANS

Amphibians live all around you, although you may rarely see them. They include the frogs and salamanders that crawl, hop, and swim though forests and waterways, and the secretive, wormlike caecilians that burrow under tropical soils.

The word *amphibian* means "living a double life," a tribute to the fact that most animals in this group live both on land and in water. But amphibians have another kind of "double life" as well—they go through a radical change in appearance between their larval stage, just after hatching, and adulthood.

There's another feature that should make amphibians special to us: they were the first animals to evolve four "legs" and lungs, allowing them to live and move around on land.

Caecilians are secretive, legless amphibians that live in moist, tropical soils or swamps.

The best-known amphibians are frogs and toads. A common question asks the difference between the two. Actually, *herpetologists* (scientists who study amphibians and reptiles) don't

# Amphibians Great and Small

In 1996 American and Cuban scientists were studying biodiversity on the western slope of Cuba's Mount Iberia. While working in the rain forest, the researchers came across a species of frog like none they had seen before. With its black body and narrow, orange stripes like bands of bright sunshine, the frog was well hidden among the fallen leaves and ferns on the forest floor. The researchers named this new species *Eleutherodactylus iberia,* after its home mountain, and began to investigate its life history. Although the frog is so new to science that it doesn't even have a common name yet, *Eleutherodactylus* is already famous—for its size. Barely half the diameter of a nickel, it's the smallest amphibian yet to be discovered.

A salamander holds the record for size at the opposite extreme. In Germany in 1725, Swiss scientist Johann Scheuchzert found the fossil of a large, four-legged animal. The creature's skeleton was so familiarly human in shape that Scheuchzert decided it must be a fossilized man, left behind after Noah's biblical flood. A hundred years later, further study revealed that the fossil was actually of an amphibian from an extinct species closely related to modern giant salamanders. Fifteen million years ago, such salamanders lived in rivers and streams across most of Europe, Asia, and North America. Today, they are found only in China and Japan, where international endangered species laws protect them and their habitats. Giant salamanders are much larger than most modern amphibians and closer in size to ancient species: up to 5.9 feet (1.8 meters) long and 140 pounds (64 kilograms).

consider frogs and toads to be different types of amphibians. But these common names are useful in describing their different lifestyles—frogs spend most of their time in the water, while toads prefer land. Here, we'll call them all frogs.

Of the approximately 3,800 species of frogs, two-thirds live in the tropics. But because amphibians can live just about anywhere humans can, people on every continent (except Antarctica) can find frogs nearby. Frogs have short bodies, long, powerful back legs, and hipbones that bend and flex with ease. The result is a lean, mean hopping machine that's as well suited to hopping across land as it is to swimming. Think of toads as frogs with thicker skin that keeps them from dehydrating, which allows them to live in warmer climates and stay away from water for longer time periods.

Salamanders and newts might be a little less familiar to you. At first glance, it's easy to mistake these slender amphibians for lizards (which are reptiles). Like lizards, salamanders and newts have four short legs and long bodies that end in tails. But look a little closer and you can easily tell the difference between the two: lizards are scaly, while salamanders have moist, smooth skin. More than 350 kinds of salamanders can be found in the world, wherever there's rainfall for at least part of the year. Most adult salamanders live on land, only returning to water to lay their eggs—but a few live like larvae, never leaving the water.

Of all the amphibians, caecilians are the greatest mystery. No one knows much about their lives, which are spent hidden under the soil or in streams in the equatorial tropics. There are about 163 species of caecilians, which look a bit like chubby snakes or huge earthworms. Caecilians are the only amphibians without legs. Because they live either underground or in water, legs are unimportant to them. They also have no eyes, which would be useless in their dark, underground world. Instead, caecilians have a pair of sensory organs called *tentacles* located near the nose. Just like whiskers on a cat, tentacles help the animal feel its way around.

It might be hard to imagine why amphibians are important. But in truth, these animals earn their way in the world by playing a number of essential roles in the environment. And they benefit humans in some unexpected ways. For example, in high schools around the world, young people dissect frogs to learn the basics of anatomy and physiology. Amphibians are used to study genetics and chemistry and to help us understand the development of embryos. They are useful in medicine as well. Mucus from the skin of poison dart frogs can treat pain in cancer patients. Other amphibian skin secretions work like glue to seal wounds that can't be stitched.

Females of the now-extinct gastric brooding frog raised eggs in their stomachs and produced a substance that neutralized their stomach acids. Doctors are studying this chemical, which may be used to treat stomach ulcers in humans. And salamanders have the ability to regenerate many of their body parts. This is of great interest to physicians seeking treatment options for patients in need of new limbs or organs.

In nature, amphibians play many parts in the food web. They eat a wide variety of insects, many of which are pests to human agricultural crops. These amphibians are natural pesticides that have no negative side effects. In turn, amphibians are a food source for larger animals. Fishes eat amphibian eggs, larvae, and adults, while birds, mammals, and reptiles consume amphibians on land. Some animals, such as the fro-eating bat of Central and South America, are specialized to eat amphibians. When frog species go extinct, the bat is threatened as well. Earth's environments exist in a delicate balance, so even one change can disrupt the entire system.

With their soft skin that easily absorbs water, amphibians are more vulnerable to climate change and pollution than many other animals. Over the past few decades, scientists have noticed a decline in the number and diversity of amphibians worldwide. Such sudden changes can be an indicator to humans of the quality of the environment. If we pay attention and act quickly enough, amphibians may help us prevent our air, water, and soil from being dirtied beyond repair.

Now let yourself be an *ecologist* for a moment as you think about this last reason to value amphibians. (Ecologists study the interactions between living things and their environments. They see the world as a big, complex unit that is dependent on all its parts, however small.) Amphibians are important because every species is special, contributing to the diversity of life on our world. They come in every shape and size and live many different lifestyles. They have been around for almost 360 million years and, in that time, have adapted to the world around them in some remarkable ways.

So now we know why they matter—but where did amphibians come from?

## LOOKING BACK IN TIME

If we were able to pilot a spacecraft that could travel back in time and hover above Earth 360 million years ago, we'd find a radically different place than the planet we know today. Landmasses weren't scattered over the globe like islands in the oceans. Instead, all the land was bunched up close together—most of it south of the equator—and surrounded by a huge, unbroken expanse of ocean. Land was the realm of insects and plants, while fishes ruled the watery world.

You wouldn't be able to pick out seasons in this ancient environment, either. Most of the planet was hot and humid year-round. Drought and flooding rainfall alternated in a violent cycle. In response, the water level of the world's one great ocean rose and fell, over and over again. Fishes living in shallow parts of the ocean and along the shoreline were strongly affected by these conditions. Competition for food and territory was so intense in this unpredictable zone that some fishes were squeezed into swampy habitats on land.

Watch a shallow pond or marsh dry up during the summer and you'll see this same process in action on a smaller scale. Early in the season, when the water is high, there is plenty of space for the creatures living there. The water is clean and pure. But when the air heats up, notice how quickly the shallow water evaporates, becoming murky with algae and mud. Imagine being a fish in such a place, struggling to pump your gills hard enough to pull

Four-legged vertebrates, or tetrapods, evolved from lobe-finned fishes like this coelocanth. Some ancient lobe-fins had fleshy fins and lungs that allowed them to survive in shallow water or for short periods on land.

oxygen from this foul water-soup. The animals most likely to survive are those that can somehow adapt themselves to living on land when the pond dries up.

This is exactly what ancient fishes living in shallow water had to deal with. Sometimes the water evaporated so quickly that fishes had to wiggle across dry land to reach deeper pools before their gills and sensitive skin dried out. Yet remarkably, some beat the odds and survived, finding a balance between life on land and in the water.

## FOUR-LEGGED PIONEERS

These shallow-water pioneers not only survived, they thrived. And along the way, they evolved some impressive means of coping with their new circumstances—changes that would take vertebrates to new heights of evolution.

The first challenge was acquiring oxygen when water wasn't available. As we've seen, fishes "breathe" by a simple process: pumping water across their gills to extract dissolved oxygen. While this is incredibly efficient in water, gills dry out too easily to work well in air. Most of the fishes that ended up in shallow–water habitats died because they couldn't breathe. A different system had to come about, or they'd never make it on land.

Somewhere along the way, some fishes evolved pockets inside their bodies—pockets we now call *lungs*, which serve to trap air. Now these former gill-breathers could gulp air through the mouth and nose, swallow it into the lungs, and absorb oxygen directly through the wet lung tissues. These former fish survived and bred, and in time, lungs were found in all evolving amphibians.

The next trick for our innovative vertebrates was getting from a drying pool to a better source of water. The champions of this skill were fishes with husky fins. Strong front and rear fins originally evolved in species that dragged themselves along the bottom of lakes and streams in search of food—lobe-fins, like the coelacanth. These fins now served as oars, enabling the animals to "row" themselves across land in search of more hospitable locales. Over generations, fins slowly developed into recognizable "arms and legs." To power their limbs, these first land-dwellers developed muscles that would be the envy of any bodybuilder. They could push off the ground (against the force of gravity) and move forward by walking.

Thus, these new creatures could not only breathe air, but also could walk on land. The first true amphibians—"those with two lives"—and the first *tetrapods* (four-limbed vertebrates) had evolved.

## MAKING GOOD ON LAND

The fossil record is like a window into the distant past. We can't see these ancient vertebrates alive and in person, but fossils give us many clues to how they looked and, to some extent, how they lived.

For 110 million years, amphibians ruled the land. Meanwhile, continents shifted and moved toward each other along the equator. At the South Pole two massive ice caps formed, drawing water from the ocean and exposing dry land beneath it. Forests of ferns and early conifers (cone-bearing trees, like pine and fir) grew up to cover the land. In this paradise, insects—ancient and modern amphibians' food of choice—grew to massive proportions. Dragonflies the size of crows and cockroachlike crawlers up to 12 inches (30 centimeters) in length walked the land. Conditions were perfect for living on land.

A terrific diversity of early amphibians is preserved in the fossil record. Some were small, such as *Diplocaulus*, a shovel-headed pond-dweller that was 24 inches (61 centimeters) in length. *Eryops* was of a more average size for ancestral amphibians: It was a fish-eater about 6.6 feet (2 meters) in length that probably looked a lot like the modern crocodile. At the grandest extreme was *Prionosuchus*, which was a sprawling 29.5 to 33 feet (9 to 10 meters) in length. Most ancient amphibians resembled oversized salamanders or large, smooth-skinned lizards. These huge creatures probably weren't very athletic or quick—but that was no problem in a place where food was easy to come by.

## COMPETITION AND CHANGE

By about 340 million years ago, a new branch of vertebrates had come onto the scene—species even better adapted to life on land than the amphibians. Now three branches of vertebrates lived on Earth: one in water (fishes) and two on land (amphibians and *reptiles*). Reptiles not only competed with amphibians for food and space—they often preyed upon amphibians. To survive, amphibians underwent some drastic changes.

Most important, amphibians became smaller and faster. Many developed color patterns on their skin, providing camouflage so that they could "hide in plain sight" from their predators. Some amphibians changed in shape as well. It's around this time that frogs started to appear, equipped with their long, strong legs that enabled them to leap quickly away from danger on land or in water. By about 175 million years ago, amphibians began to develop that looked almost identical to those living around us today. The forms they took were (and continue to be) a reflection of their rapidly changing environment.

Amphibians have been around for 360 million years. Whatever they may have given up in size, modern amphibians have more than made up for in diversity. With almost 4,500 species, amphibians have found their way into just about every environment: from ponds and deserts, to savannas and tropical rain forests and even some of the highest mountaintops.

## AMPHIBIANS ARE COOL

All animals must stay warm to have energy for the important things in life: finding food, mating, and moving from place to place. Like their fishy predecessors, amphibians are ectothermic, or cold-blooded—meaning their body temperature is controlled by the air or water around them.

During the course of the day, amphibians move from place to place in search of just the right balance of temperature and moisture. When it's cool, they might move onto a rock where sunlight can quickly warm them. Frogs tend to hop in and out of the water over the course of a day, while salamanders hide in the leaf litter of forest floors or hole up in fallen trees or under piles of rocks.

Some biologists think that skin coloration may help control body temperature as well. Because dark colors absorb more heat, species with gray or brown skin may be able to stay warm more easily. Salamanders and caecilians usually have a dark background to their skin, which is terrific for holding in warmth. Most tree frogs are marked in some shade of green, a color that reflects light and heat. A see-through creature aptly called the glass frog gets its cooling green color in a different way: it sits on top of a leaf and uses the leaf's color to reflect heat off its own body.

Bullfrogs and some other amphibians do a little dance to stay the right temperature. Pushing up on their toes when they're too warm allows air to flow beneath their bodies. When it's time to warm up again, they simply lay flat and absorb heat right off the warm ground.

# Time for a Break

In just about every part of the world, there's a time of year that is inhospitable to amphibians. It gets too hot or too cold for them to remain active. To survive, some amphibians in cold climates *hibernate,* digging deep into mud or loose soil below the freeze line to sleep away the winter. Others, like tree frogs in the northern United States and salamanders in Newfoundland, Canada, have a more extreme approach: they freeze. A chemical in the blood allows ice to form inside the animals' bodies but also protects cells from "freezer burn." Heartbeat and breathing stop completely. Then, when the world around them warms, the chemical breaks down, the frogs thaw, and all life functions resume.

Salamanders and caecilians simply can't survive where it's too hot and dry. But some frogs have found a way to live even in deserts. Desert tree frogs opt to sleep through the long, rainless Australian summer by squeezing into cracks and crevices in trees, where they stay cool and moist until the next rainfall.

The Sonoran desert toad of the southern United States has even more extreme survival techniques. So little rain falls in this part of North America that the toads spend months hibernating in holes or rodent burrows. When heavy summer rains wet the soil enough to wake the toads, out they come to begin breeding in any puddle or pool that forms. For just a few days each year the conditions are right—males sing for mates at night, and both sexes gorge on food to fatten up for the next long sleep. The water-holding frog of Australia has a similar strategy, forming an extra "skin" around itself to help it remain damp while it hibernates.

Sonoran desert toads spend most of their lives hibernating underground, emerging for only a few weeks each year to breed.

## HIGH AND DRY

In addition to worrying about body temperature, amphibians have to avoid drying out. Their skin is soft and not waterproof. It dehydrates (loses water) quickly if the animal overheats. As a group, amphibians have some remarkable solutions to this problem.

The first line of defense against dehydration is a layer of sticky *mucus* that covers the skin. This acts like a shield to keep water from evaporating off the body. This mucus layer also traps oxygen from the air, which amphibians can absorb to help them breathe. Many amphibians choose to live in moist environments and to be active only after the Sun has set. As their name suggests, spadefoot toads have digging tools built right onto their feet. The toads use them to excavate cool burrows in the sand where they can wait out a hot day or even a whole dry season.

Amphibian eggs are also sensitive to drying out, which is why most amphibians still lay their eggs in water. The eggs are like little balls of gelatin through which water and oxygen can enter and embryos' waste products can exit. Soft and flexible, the eggs can stretch as the embryos grow. They are often laid in clusters or strings, surrounded by a watery envelope that cushions the developing amphibians even more.

## AMPHIBIANS: THE NEXT GENERATION

Reproduction is one of the most important forces in the life of any species, and amphibians are no exception. Frogs provide a terrific example because they're so obvious in their mating behaviors.

If you live close to freshwater or have ever been camping in the spring, you've probably heard the musical trilling and throaty croaks of singing frogs. A male's distinctive song not only makes it clear to other males that he's protecting a territory but also attracts females of his own species to him.

To mate, the male frog clasps his arms around a female's body and holds on tight. He may remain attached for days, until she deposits eggs in shallow water or moist soil. The male then sheds sperm over the eggs and fertilization takes place. From that point, the young frogs are on their own.

Salamanders don't have vocal cords, so they can't sing to attract mates. Instead, they find each other by smell or by noticing the colorful skin patterns unique to each species. The male alpine newt (a protected species in Europe) does a dance that leads females toward his sperm sac, already deposited on a streambed.

## GROWING UP

In order to reach adulthood, amphibians must go through a physical change called *metamorphosis*. Adult amphibians can look very different from their larvae—so different, in fact, that early scientists often mistook adults and larvae for entirely different species.

Common North American leopard frogs provide a good example of amphibian metamorphosis. Of the 4,000 or more eggs each female leopard frog lays, very few survive. Fishes and other hungry predators eat about nineteen of every twenty eggs. The remaining eggs hatch a few weeks after they're laid. Tiny leopard frog tadpoles use the jelly of their eggs as a first meal and then swim for the shelter of leafy aquatic plants. There they hide from *predators* and feed on algae scraped off the leaf surfaces. At this point the tadpoles look like tiny fishes, with finned tails, frilly gills, and no limbs. The pond shimmers with their swimming masses, but as with the eggs, most tadpoles fall prey to fish. Many others die of starvation.

By the time a leopard frog tadpole is ten weeks old, its gills begin to shrink and are replaced by lungs. You can see the tadpoles popping to the water's surface for gulps of air. Soon, a pair of lanky legs begins to grow on either side of the tadpole's tail, while the tail itself is slowly absorbed into the body. The froglet adds small insects to its diet and grows ever larger. It grows to be much bigger than its parents, and then slims down as it reaches adulthood.

At twelve weeks of age, arms begin to bud and most of the youthful characteristics are gone. The young leopard frog looks just like its parents. During the next spring it will mate and start the cycle all over again.

## ALTERNATIVE PARENTING

Of course, amphibian reproduction isn't always so simple. Parents of some species guard their eggs until they hatch. In the case of some salamanders and all caecilians, the eggs are fertilized inside the female's body. She may lay the eggs in a nest, or the young may grow within her body, where they complete their metamorphosis and are born looking like tiny copies of their parents. Then there's the marsupial frog of South America, who incubates her eggs in a special brood pouch on her back.

A male Darwin's frog gobbles up his hatching tadpoles and lets them develop inside his vocal sacs. The European midwife toad wraps long strings of eggs around his legs and carries them around with him for a month or so. Female gastric-brooding frogs, now extinct, swallowed their eggs. The eggs would settle in the female's stomach to develop all the way through to metamorphosis, after which tiny froglets hopped from her mouth and she went back to eating again.

As amazing as it may sound, some salamanders have found a way to live like Peter Pan: they never grow up. Species like the Mexican axolotl, the olm, and the mudpuppy remain water-bound all their lives and never metamorphose. They keep their tufty gills and large adolescent bodies, and can live and breed without ever changing into their adult forms.

## LUNCHTIME

Other than mating, the greatest driving force in the lives of most animals is food. Amphibians are no exception. Most spend a lot of time and energy in search of their next meal.

Most tadpoles and other larvae are strict vegetarians. Adult amphibians, by contrast, are serious *carnivores* (meat-eaters). After metamorphosis, their intestines become shorter (better for digesting meat) and they grow tiny teeth. Adults feed on a wide range of insects and other invertebrates, and some even hunt small vertebrates. Insect-eaters have wonderfully long, sticky-tipped

The Malaysian leaf—frog is perfectly camouflaged to blend in with dried leaves on the forest floor.

tongues that lash out to grab insects, which are then swallowed whole—all in the blink of an eye. Many frogs and salamanders are sit-and-wait predators, waiting quietly for prey to wander within reach. Others actively track down their prey or lure it in.

Because they are so secretive, we know almost nothing about the feeding habits of caecilians. Scientists suspect that they hunt earthworms, along with insects and other invertebrate prey.

## DON'T EAT ME!

At first glance, amphibians appear defenseless. Small, often slow-moving, and without claws or strong teeth, amphibians are completely unsuited for fighting. An amphibian has one weapon at its disposal, however—its skin.

Most amphibians prefer to hide from danger or bolt away when a predator comes near. Amphibians bear an amazing array of skin coloration and patterns that make them less noticeable. Most frogs and toads are camouflaged to look like dead leaves, bark, or algae floating on water, making it hard to spot them until they move. Tropical species are often bright green, which conceals them among the surrounding plants.

Other species are the opposite of camouflaged, bearing brilliant colors and distinctive designs that make them stand out. Poison dart frogs of Central and South America are a fine example of this. They are marked in all the boldest colors of the rainbow against a black background. This warning coloration is like a neon sign flashing POISON! to predators. The skin of such amphibians releases toxic chemicals that react with saliva. Predators who take a bite will suffer the consequences: severe burning pain, nausea, and the possibility of paralysis or death.

Salamanders have a second way of distracting predators. They can drop their tails off when threatened. The fallen tail wiggles with muscle contractions for some time after being dropped and usually distracts predators long enough for the salamander to make its escape. The salamander lives to tell the tale, and a new tail soon regrows.

Caecilians have a few predators of their own, including the venomous coral snake. As protection, caecilians produce toxins from glands in their skin. A few, such as the blue-and-black-striped *Siphonops* and orange *Schistometopum* of South America, even go so far as to put aside the camouflage of earth tones in favor of bright warning coloration.

## BIODIVERSITY AND CONSERVATION

Sadly, amphibians are in trouble. Over the past few decades, many species have disappeared from places where they were once common. They are the victims of habitat loss as humans move into new areas. They are outcompeted by alien amphibian species that are imported from other parts of the world as food or for pest control. Their sensitive skin absorbs chemicals that are dumped into water or that fall to Earth in acid rain, and they are poisoned. As the hole in the ozone layer of Earth's atmosphere grows due to air pollution, the global climate becomes warmer—and many amphibians simply cannot tolerate the change.

Another concern is that in many of the places where people are now studying amphibians (particularly in North America), large numbers of deformed frogs are found. They often have extra legs or no legs at all. Scientists are still searching for the exact causes of this problem. It may be the result of pollution or excess ultraviolet (UV) radiation from the Sun. Or the deformities may have more natural causes, such as a parasitic infection that scrambles cells during metamorphosis. Whatever the cause, we need to be concerned about the well-being of these animals. Their health may very well be an indicator of our own.

A tiny nation in Central America provides a vivid example of the biodiversity to be found among the world's amphibians. While the whole United States has only 200 or so amphibian species, Costa Rica (a little smaller than West Virginia) is home to at least 160 different kinds of salamanders, frogs, and caecilians. Perhaps two-thirds of all amphibian species are found in the world's tropical regions, with more discovered every year as scientists explore deeper into the rain forests. Yet the tropics are among the most endangered habitats on the planet. With every step we take toward understanding amphibians, we come closer to finding cures for human diseases. At the same time, amphibians help us to address worldwide concerns like pollution. Most important, amphibians help teach us to appreciate the glorious complexity of our miraculous world.

# CHAPTER FOUR

# REPTILES

It's the role of natural selection to constantly rework existing species into new forms with new functions. Ancient amphibians were no exception, and their evolution didn't stop when they settled on land. Some, as we've seen, became the modern amphibians: newts and salamanders, frogs and toads, and caecilians. But early on, one group of amphibians went in an entirely different direction.

Scientists call the oldest representatives of this group stem reptiles because they form the earliest branch off the amphibian line (about 340 million years ago). Nimble and quick, these animals were entirely unique. They were the first vertebrates to live every stage of their lives on land. Thick, scaly layers of skin protected them from water loss. Their eggs were special, too, surrounded by a shell that held water inside. Stronger jaws and more flexible limbs allowed reptiles to move quickly in search of larger prey. With this combination of advantages, reptiles spread far and wide across the planet—even into hot, dry habitats where few amphibians could survive.

## SCALES AND SHELLS

Have you ever seen a suit of metal armor, such as the protection worn by medieval knights? It's not hard to imagine that the very "dragons" they hunted inspired the idea for this type of defense.

Rows of overlapping scales (much like those of fishes) cover a reptile's body. They are wonderfully equipped to keep water inside the animal's body. Scales allow reptiles to avoid dehydration even in the hottest environments. Among lizards, crocodiles, and a few types of snakes, scaly skin also doubles as armor, often thickened with bone to form crests, knobs, spikes, and spines. Like amphibians, reptiles have a variety of pigments in their skin cells that create a rainbow of colors and patterns ranging from the most inconspicuous gray-brown to neon shades of red, yellow, and blue.

Turtles have yet another layer of protection: their shells. A turtle's shell consists of two halves: the *carapace* (back) and *plastron* (belly). If you turn an empty carapace over and look inside, you'll find the bones of the spine and ribs flattened and connected to form a single, hard unit. The plastron is like an enlarged breastbone. A few turtles have smooth shells protected only by thick layers of skin, but most are covered with fitted segments (actually enlarged scales) that look and feel like tiles, pyramids, or domes. Some are marked with colorful swirls and stripes.

Together, the two pieces—carapace and plastron—provide an almost impenetrable defense. Turtles may move slowly, but they're no easy target for predators. A turtle has only to tuck its head and legs inside its shell to lock itself up tight.

## A HOLE-Y STORY

Reptiles can be divided into groups based on the number of openings found in the sides of their skulls.

To help visualize this, touch the hollows on the sides of your skull, alongside your eyes. These are the temples and beneath them are the temporal bones. The early ancestors of mammals had a single hole on either side of their skulls. One function of these holes was to provide a place for jaw muscles to attach. Modern mammals have cheekbones, bony arches through which jaw muscles pass, instead of holes. Together, mammals and their ancient relatives are called *synapsids*, vertebrates with "one arch."

Among the reptiles, we'll meet two lineages—one with no openings on the sides of the skull and one with two openings. The

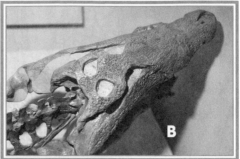

Three types of skulls are found among reptiles and their descendants. Ancient synapsids had one hole at the temple (a) (mammals have an arched cheekbone). Anapsids have no temporal hole (b). All other modern reptiles have two temporal openings (c).

most ancient reptiles are the *anapsids*, which have no holes in the temporal bone. Turtles and tortoises are in this group. They evolved more than 200 million years ago, but still look and live a lot like they did back then.

*Diapsid* reptiles, with two openings in the temporal bone, are the reptiles most people are familiar with. Many of the diapsids are long extinct, including the ocean-going reptiles (ichthyosaurs, mosasaurs, and plesiosaurs) and the land-dwelling "ruling reptiles" (rhynchosaurs, dinosaurs, and pterosaurs). Diapsid reptiles are represented today by other groups that are equally as fascinating and diverse. Crocodiles and birds are direct descendants of dinosaur groups. Modern lizards, snakes, and amphisbaenians, along with the rare, dragonlike tuatara of New Zealand, are other modern diapsids.

## THE RULING REPTILES

Many reptiles came and went over the first 225 million years of diapsid evolution. One group followed another as the climate fluctuated from hot and damp to cold and dusty. Dinosaurs and their kin were land-walkers and fliers, carnivores and *herbivores* (plant-eaters), minuscule species and massive ones. They weren't the only reptiles on the planet at the time, but they were the masters of their universe—the most powerful, awesome, and diverse vertebrates around.

Dinosaurs include some of the largest animal species ever to evolve. The long-necked, long-tailed, plant-eating *Diplodocus* is a perfect example. Walking on four pillar-shaped legs, it weighed more than 30 tons (27,240 kilograms) and measured as much as 164 feet (50 meters) from the nose to the tip of the tail. These dinosaurs didn't feed among the treetops, though. Their massive heads and long necks were too heavy to lift very far off the ground.

Despite their fearsome appearance, armor-plated dinosaurs, such as *Stegosaurus* and *Triceratops*, lived quiet lives as plant-eaters. The impressive range of weapons covering their large bodies—huge spines, sawlike neck frills, horns, and tall plates rising off the spine—served as protection against predators.

The agile carnivores, by contrast, were runners that stood on long back legs to chase prey. The smallest of these was *Compsognathus*, which was no larger than a chicken. Queen of the meat-eaters (though she also may have been a scavenger), *Tyrannosaurus rex* measured 42 feet (13 meters) in length and stood 15 to 20 feet (4.5 to 6 meters) in height. Carnivorous dinosaurs evolved impressive hunting tools: hooklike claws on the toes of their short, front legs; razor-sharp teeth up to 12 inches (30 centimeters) in length; and long tails for balance while running.

At the same time, the magnificent pterosaurs ("winged lizards"), relatives of the dinosaurs, became the first vertebrates to

# End of an Era

Chances are that several unrelated catastrophes caused the Cretaceous extinctions. It's certain that a large meteor or comet impacted near Mexico's Yucatan Peninsula around 65 million years ago. The crater, about 125 miles (201 kilometers) wide, lies below the waters of the Gulf of Mexico. Around the same time, volcanoes were exceptionally active across the globe.

Great clouds of dust and ash choked Earth's atmosphere like a global smog, blocking out sunlight and chilling the planet. Years later, when the dust settled and the sunlight finally shone through again, ice and water melting off Earth's surface rose into the atmosphere as steam. In this *greenhouse effect,* atmospheric water droplets acted like tiny pieces of glass, reflecting the Sun's rays and quickly reheating the planet. Such rapid changes would have been too stressful for many species.

Still, extinction is a natural process that works hand in hand with evolution. A family or two in each kingdom usually goes extinct every million years. Lost species are replaced by new varieties that are perhaps better suited to the changing world.

At least five mass-extinction events have occurred in Earth's history. Some scientists believe we're experiencing a "Sixth Extinction" right now—but this time the process is not natural. It's the result of human greed and carelessness: the stripping of forests for agricultural land, urban expansion, overhunting, and the polluting of land, air, and water. As many as six species go extinct every hour of every day, year after year. The loss of these organisms not only limits the diversity of life on our planet, but it threatens the future of our own species.

conquer the air. They had no feathers. Their arm bones, each with a single, long, incredibly strong finger, were enclosed in thick layers of skin that formed wings. Pterosaurs ranged in size from the sparrowlike *Anurognathus* to the *Quetzalcoatlus*, which had a wingspan of 36 to 39 feet (11 to 12 meters).

About 65 million years ago—toward the end of the Cretaceous geologic period—dinosaurs, pterosaurs, and a variety of other reptile groups began to disappear. Although most extinctions happen slowly, dinosaurs seem to have vanished over a very short time period. The cause of this mass extinction had scientists stumped for decades. Along with the dinosaurs, more than half of the world's ocean-dwelling species and a large number of land plants also went extinct around this time.

## MEET THE REPTILES

Most of the time, we can't look at a living reptile's skull to determine the group it's in. The best way to identify a living reptile is to observe its behavior and note a few distinctive body structures.

Because of their hard shells, turtles are easy to recognize. About 250 species of freshwater, marine, and land turtles exist today—from the miniature speckled cape tortoise, with its 3.75-inch (9.5-centimeter) shell, to the magnificent leatherback sea turtle that averages 8 feet (2.5 meters) in length and weighs as much as 1,300

The giant Galápagos tortoise is the largest of all anapsids and may live longer than 150 years. Today, only about 15,000 of these noble reptiles survive in the wild.

pounds (590 kilograms). Turtles are notoriously long-lived. The giant Galápagos tortoise doesn't reach sexual maturity until age 20 or 30 and may live longer than 150 years. In fact, the Galápagos Islands of South America are named for these magnificent reptiles. *Galápago* is the Spanish word for tortoise.

The 2,900 or so snake species on Earth are fairly recognizable as well, thanks to their long bodies and lack of legs. Found from deserts to rain forests, snakes may be as small as earthworms (as in the case of the threadsnakes or giant-size, like the reticulated python, which can reach 33 feet (10 meters) in length.

Still, it takes some careful consideration to be sure you're looking at a snake. After all, the secretive amphisbaenians, residents of the equatorial tropics, are also virtually legless. There are limbless lizard species too. To tell them apart, first look at the animal's head. Snakes don't have external eardrums (thin membranes on the sides of the head), nor do they have eyelids. Lizards have both. A snake's head and body are sleek and taut, and scales run in rows down its length. Amphisbaenians, on the other hand, have baggy skin and scales that encircle the body in rings. A few large scales on the head reduce resistance as they move through the soil.

Lizards are a large, diverse group. In most cases, they possess four legs and a long, pointed tail. They're very successful too. With almost 4,600 species, modern lizards are five times more diverse than were the dinosaurs. Though no lizards grow as large as some dinosaurs grew, a few, like the Komodo dragon of Indonesia—which grows to 10 feet (3 meters) and up to 364 pounds (165 kg)—are big enough to give you nightmares. Others, like the 1.3-inch (3.3-centimeter) Monito gecko, are so small that you'd hardly notice them.

The last two reptile groups, crocodilians and tuataras, look like lizards but are actually separate reptilian lineages. Crocodilians (including alligators, caimans, and gavials as well as crocodiles) live almost entirely in water. Their eyes sit atop their heads, allowing them to see while submerged. A transparent third eyelid protects their eyes underwater. The tuatara belongs to an ancient group of reptiles that was common even before the dinosaurs. Today, only two species exist, living on small islands near New Zealand. Remarkably, tuataras can survive temperatures as low as 45 degrees Fahrenheit (7 degrees Celsius), which is far below what other reptiles can tolerate. Recently, tuatara populations have fallen on hard times. Their eggs and young are a favored foods of rats, which were introduced to the islands on which they live by ships sailing from Europe in the 1800s.

## GETTING AROUND

Lizards, crocodiles, and tuataras are tetrapods (four-legged vertebrates). They walk with their legs splayed out to the side, stepping first with both legs on one side of the body, then with both legs on the other. Some reptiles are more acrobatic.

The Draco lizard's extra-long ribs fan out like wings, allowing it to glide between trees.

Tree-climbers such as the anoles and geckos have long legs that are perfect for striding from branch to branch.

Toes are important too. Chameleons have two that face forward and two that face backward for clasping twigs as they creep along. A curled *prehensile* tail, one capable of grabbing, gives them an added source of balance and grip. Geckos have their own advantage—a system of hairlike "suction cups" on their toes. With these they can scoot up tree trunks and even glass windows, seeming to defy gravity. Frilled lizards of Australia live in trees too, but while on the ground they run on their back legs instead of on all fours. The Central American basilisk lizards not only run on their back legs—they run across water.

Walking is not the only way reptiles get around. The small draco lizard of Asia has baggy skin on either side of its body, which encloses extra-long rib bones. These are the next best thing to wings. By fanning them out, the draco can sail between trees 98 feet (30 meters) or more apart. There's even a "flying" snake: members of the Asian genus *Chrysopelea* fling themselves from high tree branches while flattening their bodies, and wriggle through the air between trees.

Instead of legs, snakes have hundreds of vertebrae (and nearly as many ribs) attached to rippling muscles. By pressing one section of its body against a solid surface, a snake braces itself to lunge another section of its body forward. This occurs in S-shaped, waving motions. Sidewinder snakes, living in some of the hottest deserts on Earth, travel by making alternating "steps" with the front and back halves of the body. This allows them to "tiptoe" along while touching very little of the hot sand. Sunbeam snakes from Asia are burrowers similar to the amphisbaenians and, like them, have large, platelike scales on their heads for smooth movement under the soil. Whatever the exact mode of slithering, snakes can move with impressive speed. One species, the black mamba, has been clocked at over 11 miles (17.5 kilometers) per hour.

Don't be fooled into thinking that snakes are strictly land-lovers. With their paddle-shaped tails, sea snakes are magnificent swimmers and divers that can reach depths of 328 feet (100 meters) and remain underwater for up to two hours.

Despite their skillful modes of travel, most reptiles stay fairly close to home. They may wander across large home territories, but a few *migrate* (make seasonal, long-distance movements). Sea turtles are the exception. They are among the world's greatest animal migrators, traveling hundreds or sometimes thousands of miles across the open ocean each year. Only the females ever return to land, and then only long enough to lay eggs on their home beaches. No one is entirely sure how sea turtles find their way, although some researchers believe turtles remember underwater landmarks and recognize the scent of the sand on the beaches on which they were born. Sea turtles may also be sensitive to Earth's magnetic field, using an internal compass that guides them home.

## SENSING THE ENVIRONMENT

Like other vertebrates, reptiles have very sophisticated ways of sensing their environments. With the exception of the blindsnakes, all reptiles have excellent vision. They're equally well equipped to hear and smell.

Pit vipers (rattlesnakes and their kin) may be the most sensitive animals on land. Their name comes from a pair of heat-detecting organs—the "pits"—located near the nostrils. Able to detect temperature changes as small as 1/200th of a degree, pit vipers sense every change in their environments. This makes them capable of detecting a small mammal more than 6 feet (2 meters) away.

Because most reptiles lead solitary lives, communication is vital for finding mates. Some lay scent trails with substances emitted from glands on the thighs or belly. Geckos use their voices to stay in touch, chirping and peeping at each other through the darkness. Still in the egg, crocodilians chirp to let their mothers know they're ready to hatch. Adult crocodilians use their voices, too. Males bellow fiercely to intimidate rivals and intruders in their territories.

Many reptiles are silent, though, and rely more on visual communication than on sounds. Anole and draco lizards discourage intruders from entering their territories by spreading out colorful "flags" of skin that are usually tucked underneath the throat. They use the same approach to impress females.

### BEING DEFENSIVE

Crocodilians, Komodo dragons, and some other reptiles are so large that they have few predators (aside from humans). But among the smaller lizards, aggressive displays are important defense mechanisms. Most reptiles rely on scaly spines, horns, expandable neck frills, and "helmets" to make them appear larger and more intimidating than they really are. Widening their eyes, baring a mouthful of sharp teeth (however small), puffing themselves up like balloons, and hissing usually doesn't hurt, either. When threatened, a lizard may bite or use its tail like a whip.

Male lizards might butt heads or get into a tussle now and then, but more often they'll use head-bobbing and "push-ups" to show their strength. Snakes behave similarly, raising the upper halves of their bodies off the ground and wrapping around opponents to push them down. Even normally mild-mannered tortoises engage in battles, clashing their shells in an attempt to flip each other over.

Beaded lizards and Gila monsters from Mexico and the American Southwest come equipped with an extra layer of defense: *venom* stored in the lower jaw. Venom oozes onto the teeth and is injected as the animal bites down and chews repeatedly.

The real biters, of course, are the snakes. Venomous or not, a snake's needlelike teeth are an effective deterrent to predators. Venom, delivered by hollow fangs, just seals the deal. It's a mix of enzymes (protein molecules that prompt chemical reactions) that, when injected, attack the central nervous system or the muscles and tissues. Some varieties of venom may cause an uncomfortable but temporary reaction, while others can bring death to even the largest of victims. Sea snakes have the most deadly venom of all: a single bite is strong enough to kill several humans.

Of course, any animal with an ounce of sense will do its best to avoid a fight—and reptiles are no fools. More often than not, if a flashy threat doesn't send a predator running, then escape is the next best option. Camouflage and distraction techniques aid in the process.

The skinks, a variety of smooth-skinned woodland lizard, use color to confuse predators. Shingleback skinks flash their fleshy, blue tongues at the bad guys, and young skinks often have colorful tail-tips that are designed to focus a predator's attention away their vulnerable heads. Many lizards are able to "drop" their tails, like salamanders, leaving them behind to wriggle and distract their enemies.

Also like the amphibians, reptiles often evolve to blend in with their environments. Snakes provide some excellent examples: emerald tree boas are the exact green of rain forest trees, red spitting cobras are colored like red desert sandstone, and rattlesnakes are darkly mottled to match rocks and dried leaves. Some reptiles can even change their color from one moment to the next. By adjusting the balance of pigments in their skin cells, chameleons can match themselves to almost any background.

## A BITE TO EAT

For birds and mammals (the next groups of vertebrates we'll meet), food is the energy source that is used to create body heat. This body-warming strategy is called homeothermy, and the animals that use it are called *homeotherms*. There's evidence that some dinosaurs may have been able to maintain their body heat from within. But like fishes and amphibians, modern reptiles all get their body heat from the environment around them.

A warm, constant body temperature has its benefits—but it also uses a lot of energy. Homeotherms need lots of "fuel," so they spend much of their time searching for food. By using sunlight to warm up, reptiles avoid having to eat often and consequently use less than 10 percent of the energy that mammals do. Many feed only once every few days, and some even less often than that. A large crocodile may have to only eat once or twice a year if it hunts well.

## A LEISURELY MEAL

All turtles and tortoises are toothless, but that doesn't seem to cause them any problems. Instead of teeth, they have sharp-edged "beaks" that work as efficiently as knives. Tortoises are plant-eaters, while turtles dine on a variety of items, both living and dead. Freshwater turtles eat everything from amphibian eggs and larvae to algae, insects, and crayfish. The fearsome alligator snapping turtles have strong beaks that they use to rip off pieces of vegetation or to grab moving prey. When hunting, a snapper sits quietly on the bottom, dangling the pink, wormlike growth on its tongue as a lure to attract prey. The world's seven species of sea turtles are equally as diverse in their food preferences—they eat

Loosely hinged jaws make it possible for a snake to engulf prey larger than the width of its own body.

seaweed and turtle grasses, sponges, crabs, jellyfish, and sea stars (but almost never eat fish).

All snakes are predators and have some remarkable adaptations for capturing prey, despite their lack of legs. Prey is located using vision or, in the case of pit vipers, by heat-sensing (which is effective even in total darkness). Snakes also rely on hearing. The snake's body acts as an antenna, collecting vibrations and transmitting them to the inner ear. As a result, snakes may be as sensitive to low-frequency sounds in their environment as any "eared" animal. Once prey is located, the capture occurs either by a quick bite (with or without venom) or by putting on the squeeze. Boa constrictors are a family of snakes that kill their prey by wrapping tightly around them and suffocating them.

Snakes routinely eat food larger in width than their own bodies. Because a snake can't chew its food, it swallows prey whole. This is possible because the jawbones of a snake are specially hinged, allowing both the left and right halves of the jaw, and the top and bottom, to stretch wide apart. But while snakes are speedy hunters, they digest slowly. Strong stomach acids dissolve the prey over the course of days or even weeks. In the meantime, the snake must hide, because it is quite helpless while weighted down with a heavy meal.

## EATING ON THE RUN

Lizards, like turtles, include both vegetarian and meat-eating species. Chuckwallas and desert iguanas specialize in the leaves and flowers of creosote bushes. Land iguanas on the Galápagos Islands bite off chunks of cactus, munching them spines and all. Their cousins, the Galápagos marine iguanas, dive for seaweed and algae in the ocean.

Most lizards prefer moving prey. Chameleons have tongues that, when unrolled, may be as long as their bodies. The tongue, with its sticky tip, is used like a whip to lash out at insects. The delicate and colorful geckos are also insect-eaters, but they spice up their diet with occasional tastes of nectar and pollen. Skinks are among the least picky reptiles—they eat everything from small animals, to ants, slugs, and even decomposing animals.

The massive Komodo dragons scavenge meat from dead animals, but are fierce predators as well. Powerful jaws and claws make them capable of bringing down adult water buffalo and deer. To the frustration of their human neighbors, Komodo dragons are also fond of domestic cattle and pigs.

When it comes down to it, though, the award for Most Perfect Carnivore has to go to the crocodilian. With excellent senses of sight, hearing, and especially smell, crocodilians are ready for anything. Young crocodilians primarily eat insects but choose larger prey later in life. While most species prefer fish, full-grown Nile crocodiles have been known to take down water buffalo.

Clumsy on land, in water crocodilians are as graceful as they are strong.

Crocodilians attack by sneaking up on prey while still under the water and then lunging forward. Large teeth enable them to grab and hold prey of almost any size. If they meet resistance, attacking crocodilians begin a "death roll," hugging prey tightly and spinning repeatedly in the water. Crocodilians are well equipped with biting teeth, but they have none suited for chewing. Like snakes, they swallow their prey whole.

Crocodilians have a few interesting evolutionary *adaptations* that contribute to their success as predators. They are the only living reptiles with four-chambered hearts. This set-up completely divides the flow of oxygenated and deoxygenated blood through the heart, providing a more efficient shipment of oxygen to the body. More oxygen means more energy. The other adaptation was discovered only recently; crocodilians have specially designed heart valves that allow them to "hold their breath" for hours. When a crocodile slips under the water to watch for prey, these valves (shaped like cogs, or small teeth that fit closely together) completely stop the flow of blood to the lungs. Oxygen is circulated back to the body and recycled instead.

## THE AMNIOTIC EGG

We've already painted a pretty clear picture of vertebrate reproduction, and most of that applies to reptiles as well: male and female, sperm and egg, fertilization, development of the embryo inside an egg. Just like fishes and amphibians, some reptiles lay their eggs externally, while with others, the eggs hatch within the mother's body and she gives birth to live young.

Early reptiles developed (or evolved) some great innovations in reproduction over the earlier vertebrate groups. The first of these is that all male reptiles deposit their sperm inside a female's body.

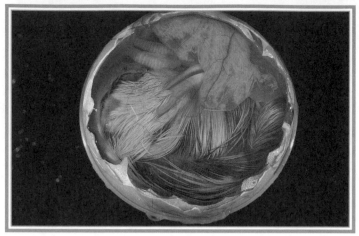

Reptiles, birds, and mammals have amniotic eggs that contain several layers of fluid to protect and nourish the growing embryos.

There are even a few extreme approaches to reproduction. Among the whiptail lizards of the Americas, some populations contain no males at all. Females reproduce by a phenomenon called *parthenogenesis*—they lay eggs that develop without having been fertilized. Offspring produced this way are essentially clones of their mothers and are capable of surviving and reproducing.

Most reptiles are fully independent from the moment of their hatching. They must feed themselves and be strong and clever enough to stay alive. The few cases of parental care among reptiles, though, are downright impressive.

Crocodilians build nests like other reptiles, but what's different is their behavior once the eggs begin to hatch. Female crocodilians hear the calls of their hatching young and rush to their defense. Calling in reply, crocodile parents dig up their buried nests and may help the hatchlings escape from their eggs. The Nile crocodile mother gingerly carries her young from the nest to the water in her mouth. Although young crocodilians must feed themselves, their parents stay nearby for a while to scare off predators. Pythons (a type of snake) are excellent parents too. Females curl around their developing eggs, keeping them warm and guarding them from danger.

# Beach Babies

Despite their wandering tendencies, female turtles are also loyal homebodies. A female not only uses a single beach whenever she nests, she usually nests on the same beach where she was born.

Sea turtles meet and mate at sea. As much as a year later, under the cover of night, the female sea turtle emerges from the water and hauls herself onto the sand, well beyond the wave line. She then carefully chooses a spot and begins to dig, using her huge front and back flippers as shovels. She will deposit 80 to 120 soft-shelled eggs deep in the sand. When she's done laying, the female stirs up sand all around the nest and pats it down carefully, making it almost impossible for predators to see. With her work done, the turtle returns to sea.

Meanwhile, the eggs incubate in the warm sand for about two months. The temperature of the sand determines the gender of the developing embryos: warmer sand produces more females, while cooler sand produces more males. Hatchling turtles make their escape using a temporary, razor-sharp tooth on their upper jaws to saw through their shells.

Just as their mother laid her eggs under the cover of darkness, young turtles erupt from their nests at night to increase their protection from predators. There's a dangerous journey ahead for these silver dollar–size reptiles. They must make it into the water, past hungry crabs and shorebirds, and then survive the long swim to offshore kelp beds. There, if they're lucky, the young turtles will live in relative safety for many years, growing large in preparation for their own long journeys through the oceans of the world.

Essential to all of this is the *amniotic egg* itself, wonderfully equipped for survival on land. Reptile eggs are covered in a strong, flexible shell that allows oxygen in but prevents the loss of water. Inside, there are several layers of fluid. Lying just inside the shell is the *chorion*, a "garbage bag" for the embryo's waste products. The thick *allantois* rests inside this. It is loaded with blood vessels that carry oxygen to the embryo. Directly surrounding the delicate young reptile is another layer of fluid, the *amnion*. This provides protection from bumps and jars that might otherwise cause damage to the embryo. A protein-laden *yolk sac* is attached to the embryo's body and serves as a food source throughout the tiny reptile's development.

## ANOTHER SIXTY-FIVE MILLION YEARS?

Reptiles provide a fascinating look into 300 million years of the history of life on Earth. Not only are they beautiful to look at, but they also provide a variety of essential functions.

Reptiles are great consumers of rodents and insect pests. They are also an important food source for animals including owls, hawks, minks, raccoons, and even other reptiles. Those that eat fruits are critical to the dispersal of seeds from the plants they visit. Some reptiles may even be the source of medical breakthroughs that will benefit humans. Recently, for instance, the copperhead snake's venom was shown to slow the growth and spread of breast cancer cells in laboratory mice.

But even as some humans are trying to protect reptiles, others are acting in ways that put them at serious risk. More and more reptiles die as we pollute their waterways, introduce destructive cattle and pigs into their habitats, and strip their homes to make way for human development and agriculture. Sea turtles drown in shrimp nets and choke on plastic trash. Many reptiles are collected from the wild to be sold as pets and are killed for use in clothing or decorative items.

Do we want to believe that reptiles will still be around 65 million years from now? Of course we do. This time, though, it's up to us to make that possible.

# CHAPTER FIVE

# BIRDS

You may have heard the old joke "Which came first, the chicken or the egg?" From a scientist's point of view, the answer is easy: the egg, of course! Birds inherited the amniotic egg from their reptilian ancestors.

The egg is just one of many evolutionary links between birds and reptiles. They also share a common digestive organ (the gizzard), scaly skin (feathers are scales that have been modified for flight and insulation), and a variety of other features.

The burning questions are when birds first appeared and from which line of reptiles they branched. There's some dispute on that subject, mostly because the fossil record is still incomplete, but there are some interesting theories.

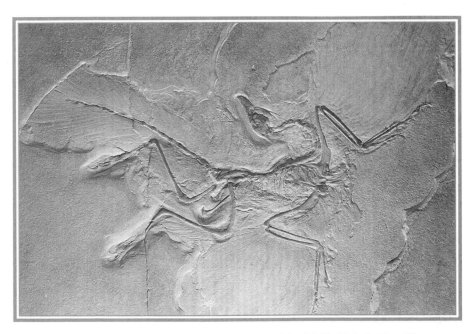

The first fossil of *Archaeopteryx* was found in 1861. This 145-million-year-old feathered reptile is believed to be the ancestor of modern birds.

## ANCIENT WINGED THINGS

The most popular theory of bird evolution involves *Archaeopteryx* (from the ancient Greek words for "ancient winged thing"), a fossil found in a German rock quarry in 1861. Scientists quickly recognized this 145-million-year-old creature to be a relative of the therapods, two-legged carnivorous dinosaurs such as *Tyrannosaurus rex*. Like therapods, *Archaeopteryx* had teeth, three claws on its front limbs, hips built for walking upright, and a long, bony tail for balance.

Yet *Archaeopteryx* also possessed some decidedly birdlike features. Its forelimbs were exceptionally long and it had a wishbone (a fused collarbone that, in birds, is attached to the wings). Most astounding, though, was that this pre-bird fossil had a halo of long feathers around its front legs and tail.

*Archaeopteryx* probably wasn't a strong flier. Still, it's hard to ignore the traits *Archaeopteryx* and modern birds have in common. For over a hundred years *Archaeopteryx* has been widely accepted as the transition species between dinosaurs and birds. Since 1999 researchers in China have identified fossils of several more feathered therapod dinosaur species. Their short feathers wouldn't have allowed these dinosaurs to fly, but probably evolved as a way of keeping them warm in a cold climate.

A few other fossil animals complicate matters, however. *Protoavis texensis*, unearthed in Texas in 1990, also shows interesting similarities to birds, but is at least 75 million years older than *Archaeopteryx*. A 220-million-year-old Asian species called *Longisquama insignis* didn't have wings, but may have had feathers. It wasn't a dinosaur at all, but rather an archosaur, a more ancient form of reptile.

With all these possibilities, how can scientists determine which of these is the true ancestor of birds? Only time and the discovery of more fossils will reveal the truth. In the meantime, we have over 9,700 kinds of birds to admire in our world today.

## BIRDS, BIRDS, EVERYWHERE

You might wonder how it's possible for so many species of birds to coexist. The ability to fly has a lot to do with it. Wings allow birds to inhabit parts of the world that few other vertebrates can reach. Birds are found on every continent and on the most remote ocean islands. Some soar over the ocean for most of their lives, while others swim in the coldest seas. The other part of the answer lies in the vast range of environmental *niches* (roles) that birds can fill. There are species adapted to eat everything from nectar to decomposing flesh. Birds build nests in trees, on cliff faces, or among pebbles on beaches. There are birds that are active by day, and others that are *nocturnal* and only are active at night.

Fossils reveal that even the earliest birds were excellent fliers. Over the course of 75 million years, however, birds have taken a few different evolutionary pathways. *Ratite* birds, such as ostriches and emus, are often large bodied and have small, almost useless wings. Instead of flying, ratites run. Ostriches, which can be up to 10 feet (3 meters) in height, are the largest birds and the world's fastest two-legged sprinters. They are capable of outrunning racehorses.

Most birds are *carinate*, having a bony extension off the breastbone where the flight muscles attach. In this group you'll find everything from sparrows and eagles to vultures and penguins. Penguins might seem out of place among flying birds, but in fact their ancestors were able to fly. Modern penguins use their small wings to "fly" through water.

## FINE FEATHERED FRIENDS

Check out a bird skeleton and you'll see how perfectly adapted it is for flight. One of the secrets of a bird's light weight is hidden inside its bones. Instead of being solid, they're like honeycomb-filled straws full of air spaces. Birds also have fewer bones than other vertebrates. They have fewer ribs and lightweight, toothless beaks instead of heavy jawbones. The many bones usually found in the wrist and hand are fused to form the wing tip.

Wings are essential to flight, but it takes more than light bones and long arms to get a bird in the air. Feathers are the key. The "backbone" of each feather is its hollow shaft. Dozens of barbs grow off either side of the shaft, like soft teeth in a very fine-toothed comb, giving feathers their structure and strength. Most birds have several types of feathers, each of which serves a different function.

Down and semi plume feathers are soft and wispy, lying close to the body to trap warm air and (in swimming birds) to increase buoyancy. Contour feathers cover the outer surface of the body and wings. These are long and strong, but also flexible and incredibly light, giving birds their streamlined body shape to assist with balance, steering, and smooth flight. Unlike down, contour feathers are "zipped" together by microscopic hooks that create a solid, yet flexible fabric.

## KEEPING FEATHERS SHIPSHAPE

With constant use, feathers wear down and lose their sleek shape. Their tips become ragged and create wind resistance. If you've ever found a feather lying around, then you've seen evidence of the *molt*, the process by which birds replace old feathers. Seasonal changes in *plumage* (the complete covering of feathers) may serve as camouflage, as is the case with the summer-brown ptarmigan's snow-white winter feathers. In spring, the molt allows some birds to take on a bold appearance that attracts mates and threatens rivals. Feathers may molt all at once, leaving the bird flightless and vulnerable for a few weeks. More often, a few feathers drop off at a time, allowing birds to continue flying while replacements grow.

Regular hygiene is as important to a bird's health as it is to yours. Birds preen every day to keep their feathers clean and neat. An oil gland at the base of the tail provides the perfect "feather gel" that, when combed through the feathers, keeps them flexible and water-resistant. Most birds also bathe either in water or (in dry habitats) in dust.

## LIFE IN THE FAST LANE

To power their active lifestyles, birds have a different *metabolism* than do the vertebrates we've met so far. They're homeothermic, maintaining a constant body temperature that's warmer than the air around them. A bird's heart contains four chambers that completely separate the flow of oxygen-rich blood to the brain, muscles, and organs from the return flow of deoxygenated blood.

Because they have no teeth and must swallow prey whole or in large chunks, or eat hard-to-digest items like seeds and vegetation, birds need a special organ to do their "chewing." The gizzard is a muscular bag that serves this exact function. Food initially passes through the stomach, where digestive enzymes soften it. Then the gizzard works like a blender, grinding food into pulp. Some birds swallow pebbles and grit that roll around in the gizzard to improve its grinding ability. The resulting mash moves into the small intestine, where nutrients are absorbed into the bloodstream and wastes are channeled out of the body.

## GOOD SENSE

Birds might not see the world the way we do, but they're amazingly aware of everything that goes on around them.

Like scales, feathers are anchored in the skin and surrounded by nerve endings. Delicate touch receptors in the beak and feet and at the base of each feather are responsible for birds' quick responses and their exquisite control in flight. A flying bird knows when wind speed or direction shifts by feeling the changes in pressure on its feathers, and it adjusts to compensate. Many species—like ducks dabbling in murky water or woodpeckers probing under bark—have sensitive beaks that can feel food even when they can't see it.

While many vertebrates rely heavily on smell and taste, most birds hardly use these senses at all. New Zealand's flightless kiwis are among the few exceptions, using their sensitive noses to sniff out earthworms among the leaf litter. Some of the oceangoing birds rely on smell to navigate. Turkey vultures and other flying scavengers can "taste/smell" the air around them and pinpoint the source of smells up to a quarter-mile (402 meters) away. Otherwise, it's vision and hearing that connect a bird to its environment.

The eyesight of even the smallest birds puts other vertebrates to shame. Rod cells in the retina (at the back of the eye) are responsive to low light, while cones pick up colors and bright light. Millions of these cells layer each square millimeter of the retina. Many nerves transmit signals between the eyes and the brain, helping birds react quickly to what they see. Predatory birds have eyes set forward on their faces and can pinpoint objects far in the distance. The eyes of other birds, by contrast, lie on opposite sides of the face. This positioning allows each eye to work independently, collecting images in an almost complete circle around the head.

Hawks gliding far above the ground can spot a mouse moving in the grass a mile (1.5 kilometers) away. Owls get a perfect black-and-white image of the nighttime world using the stars and moon as their only light sources. The eyes of cuckoos are placed on the sides of their heads (as your ears are), allowing them to see backward as well as they can forward. All this fine visual skill—three to eight times greater than yours—isn't just for finding food and avoiding predators, though. Birds rely on sight for most of their mating behaviors and identify members of their species (as well as strangers) using visual clues.

Not least among the bounty of bird senses is hearing. Birdsong and the burbling, cackling, chittering sounds of their "talk" fill the air, yet there's more going on there than sweet melodies. Birds include incredible amounts of information in each call or song and can hear minute, meaningful changes that are completely lost on us. Male birds raise their voices in song to attract mates and proclaim ownership of a territory; flocking birds alert each other to danger; and hatchlings cry out to their parents for food.

## IN FLIGHT

A bird in flight is like an Olympic athlete, making difficult physical feats look easy. In order to fly, birds have to deal with so many obstacles that it's a wonder they ever get off the ground. Like airplanes, birds must overcome gravity and wind resistance. Birds and planes both have sleek bodies and narrow wings to cut through the air. But while airplanes have engines to push them into flight, birds must pump their wings hard to get into the air and stay there.

Wing shape reveals a great deal about the flight styles of birds. The long, narrow wings of albatrosses (a) are perfect for gliding. Owls have short, rounded wings (b) for strong, slow, soundless flight.

The wing is an *airfoil*—a teardrop-shaped surface that is wider in front than in back. As the bird flies, air rushes around the wing in two streams: one over the top and the other across the bottom. The lower stream can move in almost a straight line. But the top of the wing is rounded, so air must travel farther to reach the wing's back edge. It speeds up to meet the lower stream and in so doing reduces pressure on top of the wing. The difference in pressure between the two airstreams generates lift, raising the bird upward and forward.

The shape of the wing also affects flying style and speed. The fastest fliers and those that soar or fly long distances—for instance, gulls, falcons, and swallows—tend to have long, narrow wings relative to their body size. Slow-flying birds, like owls and jays, have short, wide wings that can't sustain long-distance flight but are perfect for maneuvering through complex environments. Tails provide additional surface area and, when fanned out, can create additional lift and help birds turn in flight.

## UP, UP, AND AWAY

Takeoff isn't merely a matter of flapping. Birds need airspace in order to flap and get that first bit of lift. Some get this simply by hopping up into the air. Others must run to build up wind for takeoff. This highlights one of the reasons so many birds spend their time in trees and bushes or atop buildings: lofty locales allow them to start flying with plenty of air already beneath them. Guillemots and shearwaters use the same principle. By placing their nests high on seaside cliffs, they can simply step off the cliffs and drop into flight, with brisk ocean breezes to keep them aloft. Eagles and vultures often take a similar approach inland.

Swimming and diving birds, such as loons, ducks, and coots, have the greatest challenge getting into the air. With legs set far back toward their hindquarters, wide webbed feet for paddling, and denser feathers to repel cold water, they are perfectly adapted for life on the water, but are at a disadvantage when it comes to taking off. To get going, these species must run across the water's surface while beating their wings wildly. Loons need a "runway" up to a quarter-mile (0.4 kilometers) in length to manage takeoff.

Flight is an exhausting endeavor, so birds save energy wherever they can. The wandering albatross, with its almost 12-foot (3.5-meter) wingspan, spends most of its life in flight but rarely has to flap its wings. Young sooty terns may spend years soaring over the ocean—biologists believe that the terns may not touch land (or even rest on the water's surface) until they nest for the first time between the ages of four and eight. Condors soar on warm columns of rising air called thermals and ride the wind like surfers ride waves. Huge Vs of geese and pelicans use another energy-saving device, in which birds farther back in the formation coast on air currents stirred up by the wing-flaps of birds at the front of the formation. This technique is especially important during *migration*, when birds have to travel long distances and must conserve as much energy as possible. Some migratory flocks are so dense that they can be tracked by radar.

Hummingbirds can't avoid using lots of energy when they fly. These little birds feed by hovering in front of flowers while dipping their long beaks and tongues inside to gather nectar. The wings move with blurring speed, buzzing like miniature helicopters. Such incredibly fast wing motion (up to eighty beats per second) is possible because the hummingbird's wings pivot almost 180 degrees. To hover, it strokes the air in rapid figure-eight motions. This energetic lifestyle is fueled by the bird's sugary diet and by frequent "naps." Hummingbirds spend part of every day in *torpor*, a deep sleep in which their heart rate and breathing come almost to a stop.

## MIGRATION

Every fall millions of birds begin their ritual move from north to south. Watch your yard or a local park and you'll see birds stopping over to rest and "refuel." Observe the night sky for the silhouettes of birds across the Moon and stars.

It's not that birds are unable to endure the cold. In fact, as homeotherms, they can survive an incredible range of climates. Ptarmigans, for example, remain near the Arctic Circle all year round. Snow buntings hop merrily along the snowfields of northern Minnesota throughout the subzero winters, and penguins in the Antarctic survive air temperatures as low as −80 degrees Fahrenheit (−62 degrees Celcius). The search for food sparks migration. Species that rely on seasonal goodies like nectar, fruit, and insects have to get creative if they want to survive when those foods are not available. Moving someplace warmer, where food remains abundant through the winter, is the answer to their problem.

Migration is so ancient and vital a process that specific routes are programmed into the genes of every migratory species. Even in its first year of life, a bird knows how to find its destination by using landmarks, the positions of the Sun by day and stars by night, and by sensing Earth's magnetic pull. Preparation for migration is triggered by changes in *photoperiod* (day length), sparking an urge to fatten up for the long journey. As the days grow increasingly shorter, migrators begin to feel restless until, one night, they simply take flight and are on their way.

Some migrations involve short flights, perhaps just to a nearby site with better food resources. Mountain species, like the Steller's jay, may simply head to lower altitudes. More often, however, birds migrate hundreds or even thousands of miles, crossing oceans and mountain ranges in their determination to reach their goals. Red knots, a plump shorebird species, breed far above the Arctic Circle

# Flightless

In certain parts of the world, particularly on isolated oceanic islands, birds have lost the ability to fly. With no predators to fear and abundant food on the ground, some birds gradually abandoned flight in favor of larger body size and running skills.

Today, about forty bird species barely have wings at all. Penguins, certain cormorants, and the ratite birds (ostriches, emus, rheas, kiwis, and cassowaries) all are flightless. Penguins are an interesting case—they gave up flight in favor of swimming and diving, and their wings have evolved to function like flippers. The penguin's short, springy contour feathers are coated with an oily substance that increases insulation and buoyancy. As a result, penguins are prepared to live in some of the coldest—and warmest—parts of the world and to spend up to 75 percent of their lives in water. Oil on the feathers not only traps air, but also allows air to escape easily when the penguin dives. Using their strong flippers like oars to pull themselves downward, emperor penguins (the largest species) may dive as deep as 1,771 feet (540 meters) below the water's surface, leaving a trail of silvery bubbles as they descend.

Sadly, quite a few flightless birds have recently gone extinct. Isolated islands, once comparatively predator-free, are now home to humans and their domestic animals, many of which (like cats, rats, and pigs) are hunters. Today, about forty of New Zealand's bird species (30 percent of its total bird diversity) are endangered, and Indonesia has over 120 species at risk. The Hawaiian Islands are home to 296 bird species, but one in ten is endangered. Within 150 years of the arrival of humans on the island of Mauritius in the Indian Ocean, all the dodos had been killed off. Already, many island species that thrived just 500 years ago have become little more than fantastical memories.

in summer and then winter on the windswept, crab-covered beaches of Tierra del Fuego, at the southernmost tip of South America. Arctic terns circle the globe on their migrations, traveling as much as 22,000 miles (35,405 kilometers) round-trip each year. Small songbirds may reach altitudes of over 4,920 feet (1,500 meters) while migrating, and one Ruppell's griffon (a kind of vulture) collided with an airplane at an altitude of 37,900 feet (11,555 meters).

Not only do birds migrate incredible distances, they often do it in extremely large groups. Upwards of 100,000 hawks may fly over Veracruz, Mexico, in a single day. Researchers watching migrations on radar estimate that, at the peak of migration, nine million birds pass over the Texas and Louisiana Gulf coastline every hour.

## TOOLS OF THE TRADE

Beak design tells a lot about a bird's diet and way of life. The beaks of spoonbills, flamingos, and ducks are shaped like scoops, ideal for straining food from the water, while those of herons and cranes are spearlike, ideal for stabbing fish. *Raptors* (birds of prey) have hooked beaks for grasping and tearing meat. Finches and parrots use their strong, blunt beaks to break open seeds or pluck fruit

Shorebirds have beaks of different lengths, which allow them to probe in sand, mud, and water for different food sources.

# On the Shore

Saltmarshes and shorelines are among the richest of habitats, where a feast comes with each low and high tide. Day and night, these regions are alive with birds strolling, floating, and diving in search of a meal.

At every depth, in the water or the sand, lives a different type of invertebrate animal—from sand fleas and kelp flies to clams and crabs—and there's a bird specialized to eat each one. Delicate avocets swing their narrow, upturned beaks from side to side, sifting the water for shrimp and other drifting food. Gulls scavenge decaying plants, dead fish, and trash, while turnstones flip pebbles and probe rocky crevices for sand fleas. Plovers and sandpipers dart along just above the wave line, plucking up marine worms and insects. The adult curlew's swordlike bill, curved downward at the tip, allows it to probe for crabs buried as deep as 8.5 inches (21.6 centimeters) beneath the sand. Oystercatchers use their long, red bills to pluck clams, mussels, and oysters off the rocks, chiseling open the shells to reach the tender meat inside.

During any given season, a marsh, mud flat, or beach might be home to two or three dozen shorebird species, as well as songbirds, raptors, gulls, and others. With each species equipped to eat a slightly different food, the habitat's resources are never overtaxed and the residents rarely go hungry.

from vines. The long beaks of pelicans come with expandable sacs at the bottom for storage. The woodpecker's chisel-shaped beak and extra-thick skull are ideal for hammering into wood in search of insects. Hummingbirds have the longest beaks of all and even longer tongues, perfect for probing deep within flowers to reach the sweet nectar.

Feet are just as revealing as beaks. Birds have four toes and their placement determines how well a species can grasp, climb, or swim. Nuthatches have two toes facing forward and two facing backward to provide them with balance and grip for scaling tree trunks. Songbirds, such as sparrows and warblers, are able to grasp tiny twigs and wires thanks to their toe arrangement—three in front and one in back, coupled with a locking mechanism that keeps the toes curled tightly when wrapped around a perch. The three front toes of swimmers, such as swans and geese, are webbed to serve as paddles. Raptors bear long, sharp-taloned toes, while wading birds have stiltlike legs and long toes that are spread wide like snowshoes to keep them from sinking into wet sand and mud.

## CHECK ME OUT!

In the animal world, being obvious can be dangerous, drawing the attention of predators and rivals. Yet many birds are brightly colored, and birdsong is one of the most common sounds in nature. The payoff, apparently, is worth the risk. The best singers and those with the brightest plumage often win the chance to mate and to pass along their genes to another generation.

Among birds, females often choose their mates, so males spend a lot of time trying to look appealing. They carefully select territories and court females with every ounce of energy they've got. Red-winged blackbirds fluff out fire-engine red shoulder patches as they trill metallic love songs, while male frigatebirds and prairie chickens fill their red throat pouches with air, strutting and gobbling for the gals. Male hummingbirds zoom back and forth in U-shaped patterns, their iridescent feathers glinting in the sunlight.

Some males bring females gifts of food or nesting materials, while others design elaborate nests. Bowerbirds even decorate their nests with flowers, food, or brightly colored objects. Blue-footed boobies attract females by marching around and showing off their clownish feet. Birds of prey put on even more dramatic displays. They may flip and dive or even lock talons and plunge to the ground while mating. All of this is to prove their prowess and their worthiness to breed the next generation.

Many waterbirds mate for life and renew their bonds each year through complex rituals. Grebe pairs run together across the water's surface, while cranes face each other to leap and dance with wings widespread. Albatrosses caress each other's beaks, and swans entwine necks with grace and tenderness.

Whatever the approach and whether the bond lasts an hour, a season, or a lifetime, courtship displays serve two essential purposes: bringing males and females together and readying them to produce and raise young.

## WATCHING CHICKS

Unlike reptiles, birds seldom abandon their eggs. Even when they do, the female usually picks a nanny to care for her young. Cuckoos and cowbirds are commonly called "nest parasites" because they leave their eggs in the nests of smaller songbirds. While this may seem heartless, it's quite an effective reproductive strategy. Larger than its nest-mates, the hatchling demands and receives a great deal of attention from its clueless adoptive parents. The smaller chicks usually die, and entire local populations of songbirds are displaced by their clever parasites.

More often, however, birds are wonderfully attentive and energetic parents. Females may incubate eggs on their own or with the help of their mates. Penguin fathers often go it alone, warming their mate's single egg atop their feet for two months. Meanwhile, the females swim off to feed. Tinamou males are

Young birds, like these red—tailed hawks, must grow flight feathers
and build up strength in their wings before learning to fly.

solitary parents, too, incubating nests full of neon-green eggs laid by
their numerous mates.

Nests play an important role in concealing and warming eggs.
Most birds tuck their nests in hidden spots: between leafy tree
branches, suspended among cattails, or even (in the case of the
American dipper) behind waterfalls. Female hornbills seal
themselves into tree hollows with their eggs, while Montezuma
oropendulas build massive complexes of hanging treetop nests.
Shorebirds may lay their eggs in nothing more than a scrape in the
sand, but the eggs themselves are camouflaged to blend in with
stones on the beach. Murres nest on shallow rock ledges high above
the ocean. Murre eggs have evolved into a special shape, wide at
one end and sharply pointed at the other, which won't easily roll off
the ledges.

Birds are born into a world filled with dangers. Some are
helpless for weeks after hatching, relying totally on their parents

for food, shelter, and protection. Their insistent calls and gaping mouths keep parents constantly on the run for food. Others, especially young waterfowl, can hop right into the water after hatching, diving straight into the business of life. Whatever their level of independence at birth, most birds are fortunate to have devoted parents at their side through it all. Parents spend the better part of the breeding season providing for their young, keeping them clean, and defending them against predators. Some family groups stay together for years.

Of course, birds don't hatch knowing how to fly. First they must grow, developing large wings and feathers. Then they need to practice, watching their elders and gaining strength through stretching and flapping exercises. Somewhere between three weeks and three months of age, young birds begin to venture into the air alongside their parents. From there they'll acquire the rest of their survival skills—hunting or gathering, singing (many male birds learn songs from their fathers), and staying alive in an unpredictable world.

## FLYING INTO THE SUNSET

In the 1950s and 1960s, agricultural science made great strides in the control of insects that destroy crops or carry diseases, thanks to the use of synthetic *insecticides* (poisons). Technology seemed to be making our world an ever-better and more productive place. But biologist Rachel Carson looked deeper and feared what she saw. Her 1962 book, *Silent Spring*, forced the world to notice the long-term effects of these "beneficial" chemicals, particularly on the health of bird populations.

Carson realized that chemical insecticides spread far beyond croplands, affecting wildlife and humans through polluted air and water. When birds ate insects dosed with the most common of these insecticides, DDT, they absorbed the poison into their own bodies with every meal. Birds died from chemical poisoning, produced thin-shelled eggs that did not hatch, or passed along chemicals to their young. Carson challenged farmers and government officials to imagine a world where crops flourished but each spring was without the songs of birds.

In a sad twist of fate, Rachel Carson died of cancer just two years after *Silent Spring*'s publication. She never knew of the 1972 ban on synthetic insecticides, nor did she find out whether the birds she so loved would survive. We are her witnesses. We've seen peregrine falcons, those delicate speed-demons that dive after prey at 200 miles (322 kilometers) per hour, increase from 39 breeding pairs in the United States in 1970 to 1,650 in 1999. That same year, the bald eagle made it off the Endangered Species List as well, joining the brown pelican in the group of birds to recover from pesticide poisoning.

Rachel Carson had a quality all of us can seek inside ourselves—devotion. She cared enough to protect the future. Imagine the impact if each of us showed such compassion and vision. Imagine a future complete with birdsong and all the other gifts that nature brings.

# CHAPTER SIX

# MAMMALS

There may be no group of vertebrates that inspires a greater emotional response than the mammals. They are a collection of about 4,600 species of animals that include humans.

## COMMON GROUND

What do such diverse animals as manatees and wallabies, platypuses and pandas, lemurs and gazelles have in common? Fur or hair is a good starting place. All mammals have hair at some point in their lives. Also, most mammals give birth to live offspring instead of laying eggs. Young mammals nurse on highly nutritious milk secreted by modified sweat glands on the mother's belly. These milk glands, or *mammaries*, give the group its name.

Because you're a mammal, use yourself to investigate some of the group's other traits. Look into a mirror and open your mouth wide. You have four kinds of teeth, each with a different shape and size, which enable you to eat a broad selection of foods. Inside your eardrum are three "hearing" bones, and you have an external ear flap to amplify and direct sound into the ear canal. This ear flap is present in all but a few mammals, such as whales and moles.

Inside your body, your internal organs are divided into two cavities by a sheet of muscle called the diaphragm—the heart and lungs are above the diaphragm, and the remaining organs are below. Your heart is divided into four chambers. As a warm-blooded animal (homeotherm), your body temperature remains fairly constant.

## MEET THE GANG

Modern mammals fall into three groups, depending on how their embryos develop. The most ancient are the *monotremes*, three

93

bizarre species found on Australia and its surrounding islands, including the duck-billed platypus and two species of echidna (sometimes called spiny anteaters). They are the only mammals that lay eggs, just as their distant reptile ancestors did.

Pouched mammals, or *marsupials*, include about 280 species, such as kangaroos, opossums, and koalas. Marsupials give birth to partially developed young that finish their growth inside a pouch on the mother's belly.

Among the 4,350 species of *placental* mammals, including humans, embryos remain inside the mother's womb, where they receive nourishment and oxygen from the mother's body until all of their body parts and organs are completely developed. These include an amazing range of species, from the bumblebee-size Kitti's hognosed bat, which weighs less than a penny, to the colossal blue whale, which grows to be up to 100 feet (30 meters) long and 160 tons (162,560 kilograms) and is the largest animal that ever lived.

## EARLY MAMMALS: FINDING THEIR PLACE IN THE WORLD

Try to imagine the dawn hours of a typical day 270 million years ago. Morning sunlight has just touched the horizon beyond a North American swamp. Insects begin to buzz and an animal stirs along the shoreline.

This early riser is *Dimetrodon*—10 feet (3 meters) and 500 pounds (227 kilograms) of mighty vertebrate. Although it looks something like the primitive reptiles, this beast belongs to a different group entirely—it's a synapsid. Unlike the reptiles and amphibians it lives among, *Dimetrodon* doesn't have to spend hours in the sunshine before it becomes energized enough to start the day. A large, bony fin on its back acts as a solar panel to absorb heat. By warming up more quickly, it gets a head start over its competitors on the day's search for food.

*Dimetrodon* was an innovator, the first in a long line of synapsids. Within a few million years, it was replaced by the cynodonts, a more advanced group. Although fossilized bones can't tell us whether these creatures had fur, we can see that the brains of synapsids were larger than those of reptiles. Many scientists also believe that cynodonts may have been partially warm-blooded. To fuel that warmth, however, cynodonts had to feed more often. They evolved longer, more slender limbs to improve their running and hunting speed.

There's no mistaking the similarities between cynodonts and modern mammals. Their teeth are one good clue—they have more than one kind, which is a trend found only in mammals and their predecessors. The jawbones are revealing, too. Unlike reptiles, which have several bones in their lower jaws, cynodonts had single jawbones large enough to hold powerful biting muscles, as do modern mammals. Three bones that were part of the jaw in early reptiles are found inside a mammal's ear, where they work to collect sound waves for better hearing. Nasal passages in the skull, between the nose and the airway, allow mammals to breathe and chew at the same time, as the cynodonts did before them.

The first true, if primitive, mammals probably appeared about 195 million years ago. They survived by being nocturnal, using their excellent senses of smell and hearing to hunt insects among the treetops. Small and inconspicuous, mammals began to diversify slowly, right under the noses of the dinosaurs.

## AN EXPLOSION OF MAMMALS

By the time climate changes caused the extinction of the dinosaurs, mammals were already flourishing.

Egg-laying monotremes evolved in the forests and waterways of Australia at least 110 million years ago and haven't changed much since. Meanwhile, in South America many kinds of pouched

Echidnas are monotreme (egg-laying) mammals found in Australia and New Guinea.

marsupials were finding their places in the world. The continents, which seem so unchanging, actually move slowly across Earth's surface. When the marsupials were first evolving, the Australian and South American continents—now thousands of miles apart—sat close together, and marsupials spread to populate both. Today, they're the major mammal group on Australia and its surrounding islands, playing roles similar to those of placental mammals elsewhere in the world: herbivores, carnivores, scavengers, desert-dwellers, tree-climbers, and so forth.

Placental mammals, which appeared about 70 million years ago, got their foothold by taking over many of the environmental niches left empty by the dinosaurs. Soon after the extinction of the dinosaurs, four distinct groups could be identified (all of which are still in existence today). Bats and shrews, insect-eaters like their

# The Same but Different

Take a good look at marsupials and placental mammals and you'll notice that they show some remarkable similarities.

Fierce Tasmanian devils are solitary animals that behave like hyenas or wolverines, scavenging animal carcasses and fighting off every competitor. Kangaroos are grazers that live in herds like deer or antelope. Opossums have curling, prehensile tails and *opposable thumbs* (the ability to hold the thumb against the other fingers) for climbing as do monkeys, while both marsupial moles and shrews live underground. Sugar gliders make unbelievable leaps between trees thanks to rectangular "sails" of skin connecting their arms and legs, just like flying squirrels. There are even marsupial carnivores. The thylacine, wolflike in appearance and tiger-striped, went extinct in the 1940s, but other carnivorous marsupials—with strange names like phascogale, quoll, and kultarr—continue to hunt today.

These similarities can't be attributed to ancestry because marsupials and placental mammals evolved millions of years apart. The key is *convergent evolution*. When species live in similar habitats—for example, deer and kangaroos both live on grasslands and savannas—they may experience the same forms of natural selection and (coincidentally) evolve to look or behave alike. Deer and kangaroos both have large jaws with heavy molar teeth that are perfect for chewing leaves to a pulp. Plain brown fur camouflages both species. Their large ears can detect sounds from far away, giving them a head start when predators threaten. And strong legs provide the kick for bounding across open spaces.

Marsupial and placental mammals provide only one of many examples of convergent evolution among the vertebrates. Another example is the flippers of penguins and dolphins, which are almost identical in form and function. It's delightful proof of the reliability of natural selection.

early mammal ancestors, formed one line. A second group, made up entirely of herbivores, produced the rabbits, hoofed mammals, elephants, and whales. Next came the carnivores: cats, dogs, bears, weasels, and seals. The last to evolve were the rodents and primates.

The evolutionary relationship between chimpanzees and humans has been the topic of a lot of discussion and controversy over the years. Recent studies of DNA—the protein that codes for all of an animal's traits—provide us with the most accurate explanation so far. Although 98.4 percent of their genes are identical, early *hominids* (humanlike primates) didn't evolve from chimps. Both had the same primate ancestor, which lived on the grassy plains of Africa. Hominids and chimpanzees split from this ancestor five to ten million years ago. Many different kinds of hominids evolved in the meantime, and *Homo sapiens*, our own species, is only 100,000 to 500,000 years old.

## WHAT'S FUR FOR?

In general, mammals do a good job of keeping themselves warm. Each species maintains an ideal internal body temperature between 86 and 107 degrees Fahrenheit (30 and 42 degrees Celsius), depending on its environment and body size. Body heat is regulated by the animal's metabolism. Nutrients and fat reserves are "burned" to warm the muscles and fuel body systems.

Fur serves as an extra layer of thermal defense. Each hair grows from a separate cup-shaped follicle in the mammal's skin and has several layers, like the circles within circles on an archery target. At the hair's core (the "bull's-eye") are dead skin cells, stacked atop one another with air spaces in between. These are the source of the hair's ability to insulate. Wrapped around the core is a thick cushion of cells reinforced by strands of keratin, the same protein that builds scales, feathers, and fingernails. The cells in this middle layer may contain pigments, giving the hair its individual color, or may be completely transparent. On the outside are scaly cuticle cells, which provide a protective layer like bark on a tree.

Like feathers, hairs get old and must be replaced. Mammals in regions with warm summers and cold winters tend to molt twice a year, changing between thick winter coats and light summer ones. Those in fairly stable environments take a more gradual approach, losing and replacing hairs continually.

The winter coats of some mammals—including foxes, lynx, mink, rabbits, and beavers—are so warm that humans use them as clothing. Marine mammals (like seals, polar bears, and otters) have particularly thick fur to stave off the icy cold of polar waters. Sea otter fur is more dense than the fur of any other mammal. A single otter may have as many as one billion hairs in its coat. It's so dense and valuable, in fact, that in the nineteenth and twentieth centuries, sea otters were hunted almost to extinction.

Many mammals are covered in hair from head to toe. Short, dense underfur lies close to the skin, trapping air like a blanket. Longer, stiffer "guard" hairs are sprinkled in between and are covered in oils that resist water and wind. Quills and spines (found on echidnas, hedgehogs, and porcupines) are specialized guard hairs that are thickened, stiffened, and pointed for defense. And while the horns of antelope, sheep, cattle, and rhinoceroses have a bony core, they are covered in hard sheaths formed from compressed hair.

Long vibrissae, or whiskers, are special hairs found on some mammals' faces and legs. Vibrissae help mammals find their way in the darkness and allow them to detect even the most minute shifts in air or water currents. Look at the face of your cat, dog, or hamster and you'll see its vibrissae.

A sea otter's coat may contain one billion hairs, which trap air to keep the animal warm in icy Arctic waters.

A few mammals have taken a "less is more" approach to hair—they've lost most of it. Humans are a great example. Although other primate species are heavily furred, our hair is sparse because we've evolved a fat layer for insulation, many sweat glands that help release heat, and a nervous system that senses changes in the surrounding environment and responds quickly. Elephants, rhinoceroses, and hippopotamuses also don't have much fur. Few whales and dolphins have hair, either, although right whales and bowheads have a few hairs scattered across their heads, and humpback whales still have follicles (although they never actually grow hairs). Over time, whales have lost their fur in order to reduce drag in the water.

## OH, THE WEATHER OUTSIDE IS FRIGHTFUL

Even fur and warm-bloodedness can't solve every temperature challenge. Extreme climates force mammals to seek other solutions.

In cold weather, the first line of defense is often "goosebumps." Muscles around the hair follicles contract, making each hair stand on end to trap more air between hairs. Shivering usually follows, causing muscle spasms that increase the flow of warm blood to the skin. For mammals that live in cold climates year-round, a layer of fat can help keep warmth inside. All marine mammals (except otters) have thick blubber to insulate against the icy water. The thickness of this fatty layer varies from season to season. The bowhead whale, a resident of frigid Arctic waters, may have as much as 20 inches (51 centimeters) of blubber insulating its body.

Despite their thick fur, sea otters are vulnerable to freezing. They live in some of the coldest waters of the Pacific Ocean, yet have virtually no fat—their fur is all that stands between them and the icy sea. If an otter gets too dirty, its fur becomes matted and loses its ability to trap warm air close to the skin. In 1989 when the oil tanker *Exxon Valdez* struck a reef and spilled almost 11 million gallons of crude oil into Alaska's Prince William Sound, several thousand sea otters became so bogged down with sticky oil that they froze to death or were poisoned.

When it's hot out, some mammals (like humans) can increase the movement of heat away from their bodies by sweating. If you've ever noticed a dog panting on a hot day, that's its way of cooling down. Dogs don't have sweat glands, so they release heat from their tongues and open mouths. Red kangaroos, which make their homes in the scorching Australian outback, stay cool in temperatures up to 113 degrees Fahrenheit (45 degrees Celsius) by licking their fur to improve evaporation.

Desert mammals often have pale coats that reflect sunlight and therefore reduce the amount of heat they absorb. They may have large ears as well, which provide extra surface area for evaporation. The tiny fennec fox of the Sahara Desert, smaller than a house cat,

# A Long Winter's Nap

As winter approaches, herds of caribou move south off the Arctic plains. Whales and dolphins begin long commutes away from their summer homes in order to give birth in the comfort and safety of warm lagoons closer to the equator. Many bats seek out tropical regions where there's plenty of food available throughout the winter.

Hibernation is another option when food becomes scarce and temperatures plummet. Some bats, chipmunks, ground squirrels, and woodchucks pass the winter by slipping into a deep sleep. When the time comes, the hibernator settles into a protected place. Heartbeat and breathing slow almost to a stop. The hibernator's body temperature drops to match the surrounding air temperature. When it awakens as much as half a year later, the hibernator will have burned all its fat and may weigh only half as much as it did the previous autumn.

Bears often cozy up in a den or snow cave to sleep the winter through, although they lower their body temperatures by only a few degrees. Female black bears even give birth in their winter dens and then fall back to sleep soon after. Their tiny cubs, weighing as little as half a pound (225 grams) at birth, spend the first few weeks of their lives sleeping and nursing. Cubs grow rapidly on their mother's rich milk until it's time to venture out into the spring sunshine.

has 4.5 inch (11.5 centimeter) ears that are ideal for dispersing heat. Proboscis monkeys of Borneo have 4-inch-(10-centimeter) long, balloonlike noses that may help them radiate heat in much the same way. Other mammals get around the heat by sleeping away the steamy daylight hours in underground burrows and waiting until nightfall to emerge.

Most desert mammals have to be clever about conserving water. Camels survive in the dry desert by using their humps as fat-storage containers. Water can be extracted from the fat cells as needed. Kangaroo rats of North American deserts have evolved to survive without ever taking a drink of water. Their kidneys produce urine in a crystallized form, which requires almost no water to excrete. Desert mammals also get liquids from their food—by eating other animals and desert plants that store water in their leaves and stems.

## EATING UTENSILS

Mammals are unique because they typically have several types of teeth, each specialized for a different function. There are four basic varieties. Narrow incisors at the front of the mouth are for biting and cutting tough food. Flanking these are the knifelike canines, one on each side, which are built for stabbing. Premolars sit just behind the canines, and the square, four-lobed molars are at the very back and are enlarged for crushing. Having a variety of teeth allows mammals to eat just about every kind of food available.

Carnivores are the "toothiest" mammals. Most have all four varieties of teeth, and many have especially large canines for stabbing prey. Their flat-edged incisors are equipped to rip through skin, and the premolars are perfect for tearing meat into small, easy-to-swallow bites. The large molars work to crunch bones and pulverize meat.

Herbivores tend to have hefty molars and sharp incisors, while their canine teeth are small or absent altogether. By repeatedly crushing leaves between their large, flat-topped molars, these mammals start the difficult process of breaking fibrous plants into digestible pieces. Beavers and some other rodents chew through such hard plant material, including solid wood, that their incisors wear down very quickly. This is no problem, though. Their incisors grow constantly so they never get worn all the way down.

Some mammals have no teeth at all. Few people would disagree that the duck-billed platypus is one of the strangest mammals around. Its jaws are so unlike those of other mammals that when Europeans first saw one in 1798, it was laughed off as a phony. But the platypus is no joke: it really does have a flattened bill that looks almost identical to a duck's. Covering the bill is a tough layer of skin equipped with electrical receptors, much like those in the skin of electric fish. Using these, the platypus can locate prey even in the dark waters of the Australian rivers it calls home. The bill doesn't contain teeth, but is lined with rough pads used for crushing prey.

Other toothless mammals include the echidnas of Australia and African giant anteaters. Sharp spines on the echidna's palate and tongue work to grind up termites, and its sticky-tipped tongue is perfect for grabbing earthworms. The long, hose-shaped snouts of anteaters slip easily into the entries of termite mounds, and their ridged tongues, over 31.5 inches (80 centimeters) long, lap up the insects with no trouble at all. Aardvarks and aardwolves have small, stubby teeth—they, too, have opted for a diet of termites.

Many of the whales have given up teeth in favor of *baleen*. Each baleen plate is formed from entwined strands of keratin. Growing in rows from the roof of the whale's mouth, baleen is solid on top but hairy at the tips, and works as an excellent filter. Baleen whales feed by taking large gulps of water, which flows back across the plates and then out the sides of the mouth. After every mouthful, the whales run their huge tongues across the baleen to collect the millions of tiny shrimp trapped within.

## THE BEST OFFENSE IS A GOOD DEFENSE

Survival is the number one goal in the animal kingdom, and among mammals, every species has some special adaptation for self-preservation.

The quills and spines covering porcupines, echidnas, and hedgehogs are among the most efficient defenses. Few predators will tackle these sticky species. Pangolins and armadillos have a full covering of body armor made of heavy, overlapping scales. When they curl up into a ball, there's almost no getting through. Opossums are actors that "play dead" to discourage predators (most of which prefer live food) from attacking. Even the mild-mannered platypus has protection—wicked spurs on its heels deliver a venomous punch powerful enough to kill animals larger than itself. The spur is found only on males, however, so it probably evolved to help males compete against each other for mates.

Mammals that live in groups often post defensive lookouts. Vervet monkeys use different alarm calls to tell their troops whether an incoming predator is a bird, mammal, or snake. Meerkats, a variety of mongoose that lives in large underground colonies, take turns doing sentry duty. Standing tall on their lanky hind legs to scope out the surrounding plains, they give chittering warning calls that send the other meerkats scrambling for their burrows.

Even fur has a role in defense. It houses the color patterns that provide camouflage. Ermines, arctic foxes, and snowshoe hares, all of which make their homes in snowy northern regions, molt into white winter coats that make them nearly invisible to predators and prey. Mammals that live on the plains, like lions and gazelles, are often colored in shades of brown or tan to blend in with their grassy surroundings. A zebra's stripes would seem to make it more obvious to predators, but when it breaks into a run, those colors blend together. From a distance, a running herd looks like a swirling gray mass, making it hard for predators to see and chase individual zebras.

## HOOTING AND HOLLERING, SCRATCHING AND SNIFFING

Visual and vocal signals, along with sounds and smells, help family groups stay in contact. They allow solitary animals to locate each other in the breeding season and warn rivals of territorial boundaries.

Visual signals can be either warning or welcoming. Members of the cat family arch their backs and raise their fur to intimidate, while dogs and many other mammals growl and bare their teeth. Bears clack their jaws together when nervous, while male gorillas beat their chests. Both bears and gorillas are known for their "bluff charges" that are used to scare off intruders. At the opposite end of the spectrum, bright colors on the faces and rumps of many baboon species act as invitations, advertising an individual's readiness to mate.

Wolves and coyotes have a range of calls that express different emotions. Hyenas are howlers, too, making loud whooping calls and cackling madly. These calls carry for long distances, communicating information about food sources and helping members of a pack find each other. Most young mammals call out too. They whine, whistle, or cry when separated from their mothers and yip and growl while playing.

Shrews, bats, whales, dolphins, and elephants commonly use sounds above or below the range of human hearing. Called *echolocation*, this system of making sounds and measuring the way the sounds are reflected back helps in navigation and locating food and (at least among whales, dolphins, and elephants) is believed to have some role in communication among individuals as well.

Kangaroo rats communicate with each other by drumming their long feet against the ground. Kangaroo rats drum at different rates and in different patterns depending on what they're trying to communicate. One rhythm warns off predators and notifies fellow

The male narwhal's tusk is actually a long tooth, which may reach 9.8 feet (3 meters) in length.

rats that danger is near. Another pattern helps mates stay in touch. Yet another says "get lost" to rivals.

Mammals have a terrific sense of smell and frequently use scent to communicate. Glands that produce oils or other secretions are located in the skin and can be rubbed off onto other animals or onto physical objects as a lasting marker. Cats have scent glands in their cheeks and feet and mark by face-rubbing and scratching. Among hoofed mammals, scent glands are located on the legs and tails, between the hooves, and below the eyes. Dogs urinate to label territorial boundaries, while rodents and armadillos mark their home ranges by leaving urine and scattered droppings.

## SHOW-OFFS

Male mammals are forever working to win the attention of females and will gladly duel to prove their worth. While many fights are purely for show, they sometimes escalate into real combat.

Elephant seals wage bloody battles over breeding territories. Their bulbous noses, like shortened elephant trunks, serve as "trumpets," allowing males to bellow their anger. Even hares can get grumpy when mating time comes—males engage in boxing matches, and females may throw a punch if suitors become bothersome.

The tusks of walruses, which can be up to 3 feet (91 inches) long, are overgrown canine teeth that have nothing to do with feeding. Males have the largest tusks and use them to intimidate competitors. Hippopotamuses, too, bare their impressive tusks in territorial displays, as do baboons. Combat rarely becomes necessary for these species—the guy with the bigger fangs usually wins, hands-down. Narwhals, a small species of arctic whale, have tusks as well. When a male reaches maturity, one tooth grows through his upper lip and forms a "spear" up to 9.8 feet (3 meters) long that's used in jousting matches.

Among the hoofed mammals, antlers and horns play an important role in attracting mates. They can be small like the head knobs of giraffes, or massive like the antlers of elk. Most antelopes have long horns, while male deer grow ornate, multipointed antlers that get bigger with each passing year. Whatever their size or shape, antlers and horns are there for defense and showmanship. When bighorn rams slam their heads together, the clash of their curved horns produces a loud crack. Caribou face their rivals and duck their heads to show off widely branched antlers, pawing the ground and snorting to give their opponents a chance to see what they are up against.

## PLAYTIME!

It's always a treat to watch babies play, no matter their species. But for wild animals, play isn't all fun and games. It's a kind of school of survival in which they can safely rehearse the skills they will need to survive as adults.

The most playful youngsters are typically the predators. Running, chasing, climbing, wrestling, biting, and fighting help them fine-tune their balance and coordination and build the strong muscles they'll need to catch and kill other animals. River otters throw themselves on their bellies to sled down snowy hillsides, and badgers are known for their acrobatics. Young cats stalk and pounce on anything that moves. Although these games can get pretty rough, participants can always tell whether to take it seriously—playful mammals wear a "play face," opening their mouthes and relaxing the muscles of their cheeks and jaws to show that they're just kidding around.

Dolphins and porpoises frolic even as adults, leaping and bounding between waves or chasing the wakes of passing ships. It's not unusual for dolphins to make a toy of any floating object they find, and they even indulge in play with other species. Fast, rollicking swims help dolphin calves build their stamina. They'll need to be quick and agile fishers when they grow up. Dolphins remain in one social group all their lives, so it's essential that they trust each other. Play helps strengthen bonds between adults and brings calves into the social circle.

Primates are great players as well. Young monkeys hoot, chase each other, and swing around in the trees. Ape mothers are patient and loving with their babies, spending most of the day teasing, tickling, and touching them. Even male apes will sit patiently as youngsters use them like jungle gyms. Still, even the best parents need a break now and then. Female apes put their young in play groups, relaxing together while their rambunctious offspring work off excess energy. Young chimpanzees sometimes even laugh.

Mountain goat kids seem to enjoy "dancing" on their back legs, and young males butt heads just as they will later when competing for females. Rhinoceros calves enthusiastically use their horns to poke, prod, and push objects around for no apparent reason, while elephants slap trunks and spray each other with water. Zebra foals run and kick their legs backward for the sheer joy of it, with no idea that they may need that very talent later when fending off predators.

## THE FUTURE IS NOW

Vertebrates are but a small segment of Earth's biodiversity. Still, they are unique, beautifully complex, and irreplaceable. More important, they are the most obvious animal indicators of our planet's health.

Whatever your feelings about the natural world, it's important to think about just how complex and fragile it is. Science and common sense tell us that the species we see around us, and those we find preserved in our planet's ancient fossil record, provide essential clues to where we've been and where we're going. You may not devote your career to learning about life on Earth, but finding out what it means to you takes only a little time. Look around and discover it all for yourself.

# G l o s s a r y

**Adaptation**
Adjustments to the environment that improve survival skills

**Airfoil**
A curved surface, such as a wing, that breaks moving air into two streams, causing changes in air pressure that produce lift

**Alien species**
A species introduced by humans into an area where it does not occur naturally

**Allantois**
A thick layer of fluid lying between the chorion and amnion regions of the amniotic egg, which is loaded with blood vessels that carry oxygen to the embryo

**Amnion**
An envelope-like sac surrounding the growing embryo inside an egg (or, in a mammal, inside the uterus), containing the fluids that cushion and nourish the embryo

**Amniotic egg**
A shelled egg that allows air to pass through but keeps water inside, and which contains all the nutrients needed for the development of an embryo; found among reptiles, birds, and monotreme mammals

**Amphibian**
An air-breathing vertebrate animal adapted to live on land and in water, such as a frog, salamander, or caecilian; the first group of vertebrates to live on land and to evolve four legs for walking

**Anapsid**
A reptile with no holes in the temple region of its skull; living representatives include turtles and tortoises

**Animal**
A multicellular, living thing that eats other living things

**Baleen**  Hairy keratin plates that hang from the upper jaws of some whales and are used in feeding to filter invertebrates from the water

**Biodiversity**  The total number of unique species on Earth at any given time

**Bioluminescence**  The ability to produce light through chemical reactions inside the body

**Camouflage**  Coloration patterns that help an animal blend into its environment

**Carapace**  The bony shell that covers the back of a turtle or tortoise

**Carinate**  A group of birds that has a bony projection on the breastbone where flight muscles attach

**Carnivore**  A meat-eating animal

**Cartilage**  A flexible, tough tissue found in some fishes instead of bone; also serves as a shock absorber between joints in animals with bones

**Chorion**  A fluid layer inside the embryonic egg, lying just below the shell, which acts as a "garbage bag" for the embryo's waste products

**Clade**  A biological "family tree" that diagrams evolutionary relationships between species or groups of species

**Convergent evolution**  A process by which natural selection acts on unrelated species to suit them for similar niches

**Countershading**  Coloration in which an animal is dark on one half of its body and light on the other, which helps it to blend in with light patterns in its habitat

**Diapsid**  A vertebrate with two holes in the temple region of the skull; includes most modern reptiles and all birds

| | |
|---|---|
| **Digestion** | The chemical process that breaks down food into nutrients |
| **DNA** | A double-stranded protein that contains genes that determine certain characteristics of an organism's appearance or behavior |
| **Echolocation** | The process of bouncing very high- or very low-frequency sounds, usually beyond the range of human hearing, off objects for navigation, finding prey, and/or communication |
| **Ecologist** | A scientist who studies the relationships between living things and their environment |
| **Ecology** | Greek for "the study of home"; the science that looks at relationships between living things and their physical environments |
| **Ectotherm** | An animal whose body temperature varies depending on the temperature of its environment; includes fishes, amphibians, and modern reptiles |
| **Endangered species** | A species that is in danger of becoming extinct |
| **Enzyme** | A protein produced by cells to initiate chemical reactions in living things |
| **Esophagus** | A tube-shaped part of the digestive tract leading from the pharynx to the stomach |
| **Estivation** | A slowing of body systems that allows an animal to "sleep" through hot seasons when water is unavailable |
| **Evolution** | Change over time that adapts a species to its environment and, through the process of natural selection, produces new species |
| **Extinction** | The death of all individuals of a species |
| **Fossil** | The ancient remains, imprint, or trace of an organism that is preserved in rock or some other material |

| | |
|---|---|
| **Gene** | A strand of protein inherited from an individual's parents that determines part of that individual's appearance or behavior |
| **Genus** | A name shared by a group of very closely related organisms |
| **Geological time** | The long history of Earth broken into segments marked by particular climatic events |
| **Gill** | An organ that collects oxygen from water |
| **Greenhouse effect** | Reflection of the Sun's rays off Earth's surface and their entrapment the atmosphere, which increases global temperature |
| **Habitat** | The place in which an organism lives |
| **Herbivore** | An animal that eats plants |
| **Herpetologist** | A scientist who studies amphibians and reptiles |
| **Hibernation** | A sleeplike state in which an organism's body temperature falls and body functions slow; used by some animals to survive cold seasons |
| **Homeotherm** | An animal that maintains a constant body temperature, usually warmer than the air around it; includes birds and mammals |
| **Hominids** | A group of humanlike primates that evolved away from the other primates and great apes five to ten million years ago; humans (*Homo sapiens*) are the most recently evolved members of this family |
| **Insecticide** | A chemical used by farmers and gardeners to poison pest insects |
| **Invertebrate** | An animal without a backbone |
| **Juvenile** | A stage in life during which an animal has not reached its full size and/or adult form and usually cannot yet reproduce |
| **Larva (plural larvae)** | An immature creature that looks different from its adult form |

| | |
|---|---|
| **Lateral lines** | Lines of cells found in the skin of some fishes and amphibians that are sensitive to movement around the animals |
| **Lungs** | A pair of sac-shaped organs used in breathing, the tissues of which absorb oxygen into the bloodstream and pass carbon dioxide wastes out of the blood |
| **Mammaries** | A collection of glands under the skin on the abdomens of mammals, modified to allow female mammals to produce nutritious milk for their young |
| **Marsupial** | A mammal that gives birth to partially developed young, which then mature in a pouch on the mother's belly |
| **Mass extinction** | The extinction of a large number of species over a relatively short period of time |
| **Metabolism** | The chemical process that uses nutrients to fuel an animal's life processes and to provide energy |
| **Metamorphosis** | A change from larval to adult form that is controlled by hormones |
| **Migrate** | To travel from one place to another, usually in response to climatic or seasonal conditions |
| **Migration** | The journey some animals make to seasonal feeding or breeding grounds |
| **Molt** | The process of shedding and replacing skin, feathers, or fur |
| **Monotreme** | A mammal that lays eggs instead of giving birth to live young; includes duck-billed platypuses and echidnas |
| **Mucus** | A slippery secretion produced by some animal tissues as a source of moisture and protection |
| **Mutation** | A change in the arrangement of genes that may occur during cell division, which may result in the expression of a new trait |

| | |
|---|---|
| **Natural selection** | The mechanism by which evolution occurs, in which the environment favors individuals best suited to survive and reproduce |
| **Niche** | An animal's role in its environment, including where it lives and what it eats |
| **Nocturnal** | Active at night |
| **Opposable thumb** | A thumb that is set apart from the other fingers (as in humans), allowing the animal to wrap its hand around objects and grasp tightly |
| **Parasite** | An organism that lives in or on another organism, feeding on it and usually harming it in the process |
| **Parthenogenesis** | A rare reproductive strategy in which an unfertilized egg develops into an adult animal |
| **Photoperiod** | The duration of daylight, which changes from season to season |
| **Photosynthesis** | The chemical conversion of sunlight into energy |
| **Placenta** | An organ that transports nutrients and oxygen between a female mammal and the embryos developing in her uterus |
| **Plastron** | The bony chest-plate of a turtle or tortoise |
| **Plumage** | A bird's complete covering of feathers |
| **Predator** | An animal that is adapted to kill and eat other animals |
| **Prehensile** | Flexible and able to wrap around objects (as in a monkey's tail) |
| **Prey** | An animal that is eaten by predators |
| **Range** | The land area over which an animal moves in its life |
| **Raptor** | A predatory bird, such as a hawk, eagle, or owl, that is adapted for hunting with excellent vision and claws |
| **Ratite** | A group of flightless birds that have smaller breastbones lacking the bony projection where |

flight muscles usually attach

**Reptile**      An air-breathing vertebrate animal covered in scales, such as a turtle, snake, lizard, or amphisbaenian; the first group of vertebrates to live entirely on land

**Schooling**      Process of moving in large groups, typical of some fishes

**Species**      Any distinct group of organisms that can mate and produce fertile offspring in the wild (without human assistance)

**Species name**      The second name given to a species that is used to distinguish it from its closest relatives in the same genus

**Swim bladder**      An organ in some bony fishes that, when filled with air, prevents them from sinking in the water

**Symbiosis**      The usually mutually beneficial relationship of two organisms

**Synapsid**      A vertebrate with a single hole in the temple region of the skull; includes mammals

**Talon**      A claw; in particular, a claw found on the feet of birds of prey

**Taxonomy**      A classification system used to name living things and group them based on their similarities

**Tentacle**      An armlike organ used by some invertebrate animals for touch and food-gathering

**Territory**      An area defended by one animal against others of its kind

**Tetrapod**      A vertebrate with four limbs

**Threatened species**      Species whose population is declining, putting it at risk of becoming endangered

**Torpor**      An inactive state animals may enter to conserve energy

| **Venom** | A poison used for defense or to help kill prey |
| **Vertebrate** | An animal with an internal bony skeleton and a spinal column |
| **Warning coloration** | Bright skin colors advertising that an animal is either poisonous or mimicking the colors of a poisonous species |
| **Yolk sac** | An envelope-like structure that contains the yolk, or food source, which nourishes a developing reptile or bird embryo |

# FOR FURTHER READING

Bailey, Jim, ed. *The Way Nature Works.* New York: Macmillan Publishing Company, 1992.

Benton, Michael J. *The Penguin Historical Atlas of the Dinosaurs.* London: Penguin Books, 1996.

Burnie, David. *How Nature Works.* Pleasantville, N.Y.: The Reader's Digest Association, 1991.

Cogger, Harold G., and Richard G. Zweifel, eds., Illustrated by David Kirshner .*Encyclopedia of Reptiles and Amphibians, Second Edition.* San Diego: Academic Press, 1998.

Dixon, Dougal. *Dougal Dixon's Dinosaurs.* Honesdale, Pa.: Boyds Mills Press, 1998.

Gould, Edward, and George McKay eds., Illustrated by David Kirshner. *Encyclopedia of Mammals, Second Edition.* San Diego: Academic Press, 1998.

Mattison, Chris. *Snake: The Essential Visual Guide to the World of Snakes.* New York: DK Publishing, 1999.

Parker, Steve. *Fish.* Eyewitness Books series. New York: Alfred A. Knopf, 1990.

Ricciuti, Edward R. *Fish: Our Living World.* Woodbridge, Conn.: Blackbirch Press, 1993.

Sleeper, Barbara. Photography by Art Wolfe. *Primates: The Amazing World of Lemurs, Monkeys, and Apes.* San Francisco: Chronicle Books, 1997.

Taylor, Leighton R., ed. *Sharks & Rays.* The Nature Company Guides. San Francisco: Time-Life Books, 1997.

Wilson, Don E. *Bats in Question.* Washington, D.C.: Smithsonian Institution Press, 1997.

## RELATED ORGANIZATIONS

*Center for Marine Conservation*
1725 DeSales Street, Suite 600
Washington, DC 20036
(202) 429–5609
http://www.cmc-ocean.org

*National Audubon Society*
700 Broadway
New York, NY 10003
(212) 979–3000
http://www.audubon.org

*National Wildlife Federation*
11100 Wildlife Center Drive
Reston, VA 20190
(800) 822–9919
http://www.nwf.org

*The Nature Conservancy*
4245 North Fairfax Drive, Suite 100
Arlington, VA 22203–1606
(800) 628–6860
http://nature.org

*Ocean Alliance*
191 Weston Road
Lincoln, MA 01773
(781) 259–0423
(800) 969–4253
http://www.oceanalliance.org

*Oceanic Society*
Fort Mason Center, Building E
San Francisco, CA 94123
(800) 326–7491
http://www.oceanic-society.org

*Rainforest Action Network*
221 Pine Street, Suite 500
San Francisco, CA 94104
(415) 398–4404
http://www.ran.org

*Wildlife Conservation Society*
2300 Southern Boulevard
Bronx, NY 10460
(718) 220–5111
http://wcs.org

*YMCA Earth Service Corps*
National Resource Center
909 Fourth Avenue
Seattle, WA 98104
(800) 733–YESC
http://www.yesc.org

## RELATED INTERNET SITES

*Animal Diversity Web, from The University of Michigan's Museum of Zoology:*
http://animaldiversity.ummz.umich.edu/index.html
*This site contains in-depth information on both vertebrates and invertebrates, with up-to-date systematics and life histories.*

*Crocodilians: Natural History and Conservation*
http://crocodilian.com/
*This site is a terrific, comprehensive source on the behavior, biology, and conservation of all twenty–three crocodilian species.*

*Evolution on the Web for Biology Students*
http://www.iup.edu/~rgendron/bi112-a.htmlx
*Developed for college students studying evolution, this site is complex but is helpful for clarifying concepts and exploring evolution in greater detail.*

*Geologic Time*
http://www.ucmp.berkeley.edu/exhibit/geology.html
*Here you'll find a review of the Earth's time line from UC Berkeley's excellent Museum of Paleontology website.*

*Geologic Time, Online Edition*
http://pubs.usgs.gov/gip/geotime/
*This site offers a close-up look at geologic time from the United States Geologic Survey.*

*North American Reporting Center for Amphibian Malformations*
http://www.npwrc.usgs.gov/narcam/
*This very complete look at the trend in amphibian malformations includes an online identification key to American and Canadian species.*

## Peterson Online
http://www.petersononline.com/
*This world-class website is on birds, published by one of the top authorities on North American birds.*

## TurtleTrax
http://www.turtles.org/
*This site contains facts and resources on the turtles of the world.*

## University of California's Museum of Paleontology Web Lift— Introduction to Vertebrates:
http://www.ucmp.berkeley.edu/vertebrates/vertintro.html
*This site is a great source of information about geologic time and evolution, with terrific graphics and detailed information.*

## Vertebrate Zoology Links by Taxon, from Old Dominion University
http://www.lions.odu.edu/~kkilburn/vzlinks.htm#top
*Here is a terrific set of links that are perfect for students seeking detailed information on a particular group.*

# INDEX

## ABOUT THE AUTHOR

Christine Petersen is a biologist and educator who has spent much of her career studying the behavior and ecology of bats. When she isn't in the classroom or doing research, Ms. Petersen enjoys talking about nature with visitors in her local parks and writing about her favorite wild animals and wild places. She is also the co-author of several books in The Children's Press True Books series. Ms. Petersen makes her home on a lake near Minneapolis, Minnesota.